CPSIA information can be obtained
at www.ICGtesting.com
Printed in the USA
LVOW05s0219140218
566538LV00036B/1269/P

9 781929 133864

Tiger Tales:

The Story of the Paradise Village Bengals

By: Deborah Scott

Tiger Tales:
The Story of the Paradise Village Bengals

All original material Copyright © 2011 Deborah Scott

Published by Aventura Press

Orders, inquiries, and correspondence should be addressed to:

Aventura Press
www.aventurapress.us
Printed in the United States

First Edition, September, 2015 10 9 8 7 6 5 4 3 2 1
ISBN 978-0-9839179-0-8
Original cover design by Carroll Eristhee
Cover revision and interior book design by Eric Schuyler
Iridescent Orange Press

Acknowledgements:

To Graziano Sovernigo for his vision and inspiration, and to the Paradise Village staff who have proven that desire to make something happen can make all the difference.

To the people who shared their stories: Graziano Sovernigo, Dr. Alberto Cervantes, and Juan Diaz.

To visitors and locals who have shared their photos: Robert Pattison, Barbara Sullivan, Camie Davies, Kelly Hansen, Judy Roush, Trish Cosulich, and Paul Weinroth.

To Sonja Struthers for lighting the way. To Paula Miles, Kathleen Jensen, and David hall for their editorial and moral support. To Eric "Kata" Schuyler for his brilliance and patience.

But most of all, thank you to Jesus and Mary Carmona, who not only shared their photographs and stories, but opened their hearts and home to me during the writing of this book.

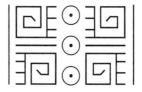

"When I see all the beauty in the world, I know God must be an artist.
And if He is an artist, the tiger is one of His masterpieces."

- Jesus Carmona

Contents

Leoncio: The First Tiger in Paradise 1

The Economics of Extinction 5

The Bengal Program's (Human) Cast of Characters..............10

Graziano Sovernigo (Don Graziano)..12

Jesus Carmona 16

Mary Carmona 21

Gonzalo Calderon 25

Alberto Cervantes 28

Juan Diaz 31

A Mate For Leoncio: Finding Casimira....................................35

The First Cubs Arrive in Paradise Village 38

Cats in *The Jungle*..42

Tiger Saves Man's Life...45

Life with Diego 48

Diego and the Great Escape(s) 53

Babes in Paradise..57

The Arrival of Khan 63

The Science of Extinction 67

Zookeeper Down! 70

Mary Meets Nala...73

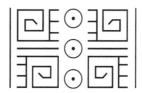

Living La Vida El Tigre 76

Lluvia's Kodak Moment 79

Lluvia Meets "Daddy's New Girlfriend" 81

A Tragic Mistake is Made 83

Daisy, the Sweetheart of Paradise.....................................87

Nap Time 90

Chloe is Born...95

Carmona's Condo That Same Night 99

Chloe's Brush with the Law 102

Chloe's Identity Crisis 105

Living in a Fish Bowl 111

Chloe Becomes a Working Girl 115

Chloe and the Paparazzi 119

For Zoe 122

The Perils of Miscommunication 129

Chloe is Transferred 133

The Ecology of Extinction 140

Heard at the Cages...143

Fierce Predators 169

Author's Update, July 2015..175

References 178

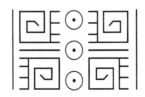

Leoncio: The First Tiger in Paradise

Leoncio cools off in his waterfall.

North of the Mexican city of Puerto Vallarta, in the state of Nayarit, is a place called Paradise. Surrounded by coco palms and *palapas*, this collection of hotel towers, condos, villas, and golf course residences is nestled in the right angle created by a world-class marina and the Pacific Ocean. This exotic setting is not only a place for vacationers to rest and relax, it is also home to several Bengal tigers. This is the story of how these tigers came to live in Paradise Village.

In many exotic feline compounds, the first residents are *rescues*. Many come from homes where well-meaning but uninformed owners thought it would be fun to have a leopard in the backyard, or a tiger by the swimming pool. In other cases, owners are hungry for power and think an exotic feline will get them respect by association. These are the cases where tigers and other exotic felines are the most abused.

Graziano Sovernigo, the owner and developer of Paradise Village, had a very clear vision of paradise, "It's a place where animals could find a safe haven living among humans, and humans could rediscover their relationship with all living things through their encounters with these animals."

In 1996, Sovernigo got a call from the governor of Nayarit. The state police had raided the house of a drug dealer and found not only drugs, but information on a four-month-old Bengal tiger that had been left at a veterinarian's office in Guadalajara. The cub had been beaten, stopped eating, and had become malnourished. The vet determined the tiger was suffering from kidney problems, but after treatment the cub was rallying and beginning to eat again. With the tiger's owner in jail, the vet needed to find a home for the cub or euthanize him. That's when the governor of Nayarit got involved.

The governor had heard that Sovernigo was considering a zoo of some sort for his new development in Nuevo Vallarta. He admitted that the cub was very weak and might not be able to survive the effects of its horrible past, but was it possible that Paradise Village would be interested in taking this tiger? While Sovernigo had envisioned a place where exotic animals could roam free, all he had at that time were three deer, which had been donated by a member of the Paradise Village housekeeping staff.

Questions flooded Sovernigo's mind. How do we take care of a tiger? What do we feed it? Where do we keep it? How do we find a vet who knows anything about tigers? All of these questions needed only one answer.

The governor was calling.

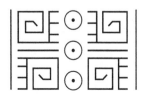

Sometimes, when opportunity knocks, you have to open the door before you're really ready. The first thing Sovernigo did was take construction workers off their task of building the hotel's main tower, and set them to work building a tiger cage. Within days, Paradise Village took delivery on Leoncio, the drug lord's Bengal tiger cub.

The second task was to find a veterinarian with tiger experience. That was a tall order in a country where there are no tigers. After phone calls, meetings, and interviews, the closest Sovernigo could come to a tiger veterinarian was a doctor in Tepic who was "good with cows."

Dr. Gonzalo Calderon, who spoke only Spanish, found that most of the books on tigers were written in English. He admits there were a few times when the language barrier caused mistakes, but his dedication to oversee a successful tiger breeding program brought him through the rough times.

That was the rocky beginning of the Bengal breeding program that produced the family of tigers you see today at the resort and golf course. The hope is that the story of these animals will educate visitors about the price of extinction and inspire them to become involved in the preservation of all endangered species.

The Economics of Extinction

From the late 1800's to mid 1900's, Bengal tigers were hunted for their heads, which looked impressive on a wall of mounted big game trophies. The Bengal is the second largest tiger subspecies, and the largest of all the warm weather tigers, so it became the hunters' primary target. As the Bengal numbers dwindled, they ended up on the endangered species list and reserves were established in India to protect and replenish the breed. In the past few decades, India reported over 4,000 Bengals in their reserves. Happily, the Bengal was moved to a lower, less threatened position on the endangered species list. However in recent years a more exacting count was done. The shocking news was that the total Bengal population in these reserves was less than 1,500. Once again, the Bengal tiger advanced up the endangered species list.

How can there be such a disparity in the numbers? First of all, it's hard to get an accurate count of tigers because they hide very well. When Paradise Village visitors have gone to the El Tigre Golf Course to see new babies, they would scan the area for a glimpse of the cubs. Some walk away disappointed. It takes a careful eye to see sleeping cubs lying in the open grass under the mottled shade of the trees. Adult tigers in the wild hide in the shade of bushes and lie still for hours at a time. They also change hiding places and dens often, so an accurate count is next to impossible.

But the primary reason why the Bengal population had decreased so drastically is that they are still being hunted in the wild and poached on the reserves. This brings us to the economics of supply and demand; fewer tigers means they're even more valuable.

While humans no longer prize the tiger head mounted on the wall, or the tiger skin rug in front of the fireplace, the tiger holds an important place in Asian medicine. The book *Herbal Encyclopedia* offers 461 Chinese medicines that include various animal parts. In today's world the tiger isn't hunted as a trophy; it's hunted for its hair, whiskers, heart, liver, muscle, teeth, claws, and bones. These are mixed into cures for an array of ills: swelling, fatigue, headaches, weakness, depression, and impotence. When Man believes an animal's body parts will make him healthier, the animal doesn't stand much of a chance.

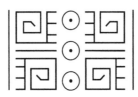

A visitor snapped this photo of Lluvia systematically moving her cubs from one area of her cage to another. In the wild, tigresses move their cubs frequently.

Secondly, killing an endangered Bengal is illegal, which makes those body parts harder to obtain, so the price of a Bengal goes up.

Thirdly, many of the dwindling numbers are kept on reserves. Now the price skyrockets.

Lastly, the areas around the reserves are steeped in poverty. The money begins to flow: from the buyer, to the poacher, to the employee in the reserve. It's easy for us to condemn the corruption, but for

Lluvia washes her cubs after they have come in contact with humans.

the people involved—from the patient seeking a cure to the poacher collecting his money—it's all about survival, and the Bengal loses.

Economists have had the most recent suggestions for ways to break this tragic chain of events. Their focus has been on the weakest link: the poverty surrounding the reserves. One solution they have proposed is to raise the local residents' farming and ranching production so they would be less susceptible to bribes.

Another possibility is to include locals in commercial opportunities so they can make money as a result of the reserve. This would not only raise the income level for people in the surrounding villages, but also give them a sense of pride and ownership in the reserve.

Whatever is decided, the worst of the battle will be ahead: imposing change on cultures with longtime traditions. Will families who have been farming for generations be able to change? Will desperate patients stop seeking tiger organs to cure their ills? The fate of the Bengal will rest in the answers to these questions. 🐾

The Bengal Program's (Human) Cast of Characters

Raising the Paradise Village Bengals takes an enormous amount of commitment: the most obvious is time. Raising a Bengal tiger cub is more exhausting than caring for a human baby. A cub feeds every two to three hours, and feeding time can take an hour. When the cub is awake and on the prowl, its human parent has to watch it constantly. When the cub is asleep, the human parent mops the floor, cleans the rugs, washes loads of towels, and researches tiger information through books, the Internet, or phone calls.

The second commitment is physical. A cub's claws are sharper than a kitten's and when the cub is feeding, its claws knead, scratch, and puncture. At three months old, a cub is eating raw chicken: bones, cartilage, and all. Just like human babies, cubs explore the world through their mouths. A curious cub's bite can break a finger or slice through skin and muscle down to the bone. Though small in size, cubs have heavy bones and powerful muscles; a stubborn cub in the throes of a temper tantrum has to be contained without causing injury to the caretaker.

The third commitment is money. Food is an obvious expense. A grown tiger can eat ten to twenty pounds of meat at a meal. But providing a proper habitat is also very important. Fresh water in the form of pools and waterfalls keep them cool and hydrated. Shade trees and grassy areas inside the cages need to be cared for and the concrete walkways and platforms must be scrubbed, hosed down, and kept clean. Zookeepers are always close by, watching the tigers as well as cleaning the cages. At night, security guards patrol the cages to make sure the tigers are doing well.

The fourth commitment to a tiger program is heart. The humans responsible for the Bengal program at Paradise Village have had a passion for what they do and are happy to share their experiences with others.

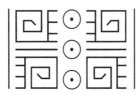

Graziano Sovernigo
(Don Graziano)

Graziano Sovernigo with a rescued owl.

As a visitor in Paradise Village, the first thing you hear about Graziano Sovernigo is his ambition as a child. He left Italy for Canada at seventeen and arrived in New Brunswick with only ten dollars in his pocket. He took a job as a coal miner and began his climb from coal to concrete, eventually developing and constructing concrete buildings. Sovernigo's fortune was made in Canada, but he wasn't done working.

He moved his family to Mexico where he developed Paradise Village. The collection of hotel towers, condos, and marina residences

didn't happen overnight. Sovernigo's key to success was to start slowly and only build what he could fill. While many people think Tower One--the Tikal Tower--was the first built, Tower Two, the Uxmal, was first. Sovernigo offered cruise ship lines a land excursion to play on the beach and enjoy a poolside buffet. As word spread about the resort, the Tikal Tower was built to accommodate the growth in business.

But Sovernigo wanted this development to be something more than a resort. He wanted it to embody paradise, a place where people and animals could live together. When he took delivery on his first two ostriches, he allowed them to roam the grounds and explore the beach. That is until one of the ostriches developed a fascination for the nail polish on the fingers of a sleeping beachgoer. The bird began pecking and pulling at the woman's fingers until she woke from her dreamy sleep to find herself staring into the eye of an ostrich. She screamed in horror, which startled the bird, and that panicked everyone else on the beach. After the commotion died down, it was decided the ostriches would have human attendants to keep them from trying to steal polished fingernails.

The Paradise Village Zoo is an example of Sovernigo's commitment to the animal life of the area. All the species are local animals that have been found injured or dropped off by locals hoping that Sovernigo's vets and staff will be able to heal them. They have treated crocodiles, raccoons, deer, and many different species of birds from pelicans to flamingos.

With the slow and methodic growth of Paradise Village, Sovernigo had time to develop business relationships with the locals, as well as state and federal officials. As a tribute to his wealth and power, the locals respectfully refer to him as *Don Graziano*.

He has also given back to the human community in many ways: providing jobs, assistance, and opportunities for new businesses, as well as encouraging legal and medical professionals to come to Nuevo Vallarta.

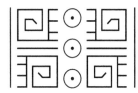

Through a charitable foundation called Families at the Dump, he donates food, clean water, and medical care to two hundred fifty people who live in the dump at Puerto Vallarta. To help break the cycle of poverty, this foundation also provides education to the children in these families. Recent high school graduates are now attending universities throughout the country.

The Paradise Village Bengal Tiger Program is just one of his many projects, but he has always been devoted to it. Whatever the tigers have needed for their comfort or health has been readily provided by Don Graziano. From the beginning, he has funded every aspect of the program which allows Bengal tigers to be placed in zoos and habitats so people can enjoy them, learn from them, and help these magnificent animals avoid extinction.

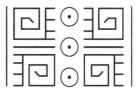

Jesus Carmona

Jesus Carmona with five-month-old Chloe.

When it comes to caring for animals, there are two kinds of people: *animal* people and *people* people. *Animal* people are consumed with the animals they care for. They seem to have a sixth sense about animals and feel a sense of peace they get nowhere else. Because of this comfort level, they would often rather be with their animals because they feel a closeness they don't have with humans. Animal people often choose careers in veterinary science, animal behavior, zookeeping, animal training, or even K-9 police work.

People people love animals. They care for them, give them good homes, and are very responsible. But they also feel a closeness with humans. Their intuition connects to human needs and desires. They feel empathy with humans and are great communicators and teachers because they know how to relate to people.

Jesus Carmona, the director of the Paradise Village Bengal Tiger Program was both. His keen awareness of tiger behavior and his love of teaching enabled him to work with both tigers and people.

His unusual upbringing was the key to his talents.

Carmona was born in Acapulco: Mexico's most popular tourist destination at the time. Acapulco was not only known for its parasailing and cliff-diving, but for its red-hot night clubs with thumping music and dancing until dawn. As a boy, Carmona was fascinated by the people who partied in the clubs. By the time he was a teen, he had worked his way into the club scene and was a popular deejay. He saw that speaking English was a great way to meet girls, but he was no longer in school and certainly couldn't afford private lessons. So he developed his own way to learn English. He memorized the lyrics to the songs he played in the clubs.

To this day he has a fondness for Gino Vannelli's song, "Lady," because the lyrics were particularly successful with all the ladies.

Over the years, his work in clubs grew from deejay to manager, and he ended up running a club in Houston, Texas. One of his friends worked with the tigers at the Houston Zoo and invited Carmona to visit behind the scenes. Carmona was fascinated by the Bengal tigers: their power, their grace, and regal bearing. It was the beginning of many trips to the zoo to watch the tigers and ask endless questions about their behavior and the care they received. Night clubs were Carmona's career, but tigers became his passion. His time away from the club was spent reading books about tigers and visiting other zoos to tour tiger facilities.

Meanwhile, in Mexico, the cities on the Mexican Riviera—Cabo San Lucas, Puerto Vallarta, and Mazatlan—were emerging as the hot

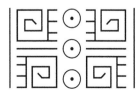

tourist spots with night clubs popping up everywhere. Carmona moved to Puerto Vallarta to manage a club, which became a very popular night spot. Even at this point in his life he held tight to his fascination with Bengal tigers. He kept in touch with the friends he'd made at American zoos and spent his vacations visiting the tigers and their caretakers.

On one visit, he stayed in Houston to visit the zookeepers and observe the tigers while his wife went to the east coast to visit family. Tragically, she was killed in a car accident. After the funeral, a devastated Carmona returned to his club in Puerto Vallarta. He poured his time and energy into his work, trying to move on. The club was a huge success. Everyone seemed to know Carmona and his talent for creating a good time for his guests. But privately, the death of his wife had left him empty and made him question what he should do with the rest of his life.

In Nuevo Vallarta, Graziano Sovernigo was ready to develop the next phase of Paradise Village. Construction was moving forward to build Xcaret as an on-site night club/disco, and plans were being discussed for a restaurant/night club to be located in the Paradise Village Mall. Don Graziano needed a manager who understood the food and beverage business as well as the entertainment business. He heard of Carmona's popularity in Puerto Vallarta and offered him the job.

For Carmona the offer meant a new start. He liked the prospect of being included in the development phase of two night clubs, but Paradise Village had something else to offer: Leoncio, the Bengal tiger cub who was now eight months old. Don Graziano's plan was to acquire a female, breed some tigers, and place them on the grounds of the future El Tigre Golf Course where Carmona would supervise the program.

In that one job offer, Carmona saw both his career and his passion merge into one life path. He could be with people in the clubs and be close to tigers. He took the job and made arrangements to move to

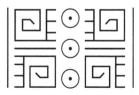

19

Paradise Village. There, he joined other employees who lived in a row of small apartments where the Tonina Tower now stands.

The club in Puerto Vallarta threw a huge farewell party for Carmona. Between the food, drinks, and non-stop music, the crowd partied most of the night. Then Carmona drove to Paradise Village to start his new life. He sat in his car looking into the barren field that lay ahead and thought about this tremendous opportunity he had been given.

Paradise Village was big and getting bigger every week. Everyone talked about how organized the development was and how things ran so smoothly. He looked forward to being a part of something larger than just a night club. And his previous experience with zoos made him ready to tackle any challenge the tiger program would present.

Suddenly he heard voices in the distance and saw the glow of flashlights heading toward his car. As the figures got closer, he realized they were Paradise Village security guards sprinting across the field in a state of worry and panic. He asked them where they were going. One of the guards stopped long enough to tell him that someone had forgotten to close the cage door at the animal compound and a deer had escaped. It was up to five security guards with flashlights and ropes to catch it.

Carmona sat in his car and watched them run through the field, then he stared into the pre-dawn grey sky. Someone left an animal's cage door open? What if it had been Leoncio's cage?

Maybe there would be more to this job than he realized. 🐾

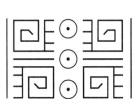

Mary Carmona

Mary Carmona celebrating Chloe's first Christmas.

Mary Carmona, a native of Ohio, had a father who was raised on a five-hundred acre farm. Mary says that even though she grew up in a suburb of Cincinnati, her father acted like he had never left that farm.

He worked for the University of Cincinnati, as the head of heating and refrigeration in the building that housed the Kettering animal testing lab. When the lab conducted tests on a group of animals, it was common procedure to euthanize all the animals involved once the testing was finished. For instance, if the university was testing a newly

developed vaccine on fifty lab mice, they would put a spot of orange dye on the fur of the twenty-five mice in the control group and a spot of yellow on the twenty-five mice receiving the vaccine. When the tests were concluded, it was not practical to find homes for fifty mice, so they were put to sleep.

At least, that's how it worked until Mary's father showed up. He couldn't bear to see an animal disposed of when all it needed was a good home. So he provided one. The backyard became a makeshift petting zoo, and the garage was transformed into a chicken coop.

Thanks to her father's fondness for doomed lab animals, Mary's childhood was a colorful one. She played with rats and mice that had bright dye spots on their coats. There were guinea pigs with blue or pink polka dots, goats with a stripe of orange or green across their ribs, ducks with purple feathers, and bunnies of every color imaginable. She didn't know what the dye spots were for, she just thought they were pretty. Mary was knee deep in animals and loved every minute of it.

Her mother was a homemaker who had her work cut out for her taking care of the family zoo. One of Mary's favorite memories was her mother's birthday when her dad brought home two hundred baby chicks. Looking back she laughs, "God knows what we were exposed to, playing with lab animals." As she grew up, Mary found herself rescuing animals and nursing them back to health.

She met Carmona after his wife died; she was vacationing in Puerto Vallarta and visited his restaurant. When she returned to the United States they became long-distance friends. When Carmona moved to Paradise Village and was searching for tiger experts, Mary suggested the Cincinnati Zoo. They were known for their Bengal tigers—in fact, that's how the Cincinnati football team had gotten its name.

Thanks to Mary's suggestions, Carmona was soon talking regularly to Mike Dulaney of the Cincinnati Zoo. Dulaney remained their go-to expert for years.

After Carmona and Mary wed, she became a part of the tiger-raising team: making and dispensing formula, walking the cubs,

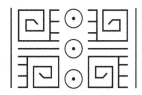

and educating Paradise Village guests about Bengal tigers. She has cheerfully endured being "pooped on, peed on, and thrown-up on."

When a cub is sick, Mary is fiercely protective and is dedicated to keeping the animal comfortable and cared for. When death is inevitable for a newborn tiger, Mary takes the ailing cub home with her. She sings and talks to it, feeds it, and lets it sleep on the bed between Carmona and her. In her words, "No baby is going to leave this world without knowing that it was loved."

She's very definitely her father's daughter.

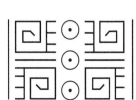

Gonzalo Calderon

Dr. Gonzalo Calderon (left), the first veterinarian for the tiger program. Pictured with Jesus Carmona and Jose Alberto Cervantes.

Dr. Gonzalo Calderon was an excellent veterinarian who taught classes at the university in Tepic, Nayarit. He came highly recommended for his skill and knowledge of farm animals. But there was something else he had to have for the Bengal program: determination.

Calderon spoke no English, which was fine when he researched farm animals and could get information written in Spanish. But the Bengal tiger lives in India, and the research is written in English.

Though highly regarded by the Spanish speakers in his field, he had to struggle for new information on an unfamiliar animal in a language he didn't understand.

Dr. Calderon poured over the text books on tigers with a Spanish/English dictionary at his side. There was much he had to learn but he did it courageously.

Without Dr. Calderon, Juan Diaz wouldn't have been the zookeeper. Juan was promoted from his position as a gardener to be Calderon's assistant. Without Dr. Calderon the Bengal program would not have acquired Dr. Alberto Cervantes, the highly skilled and compassionate veterinarian who was one of Calderon's students, and his successor in the Bengal program.

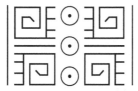

Alberto Cervantes

Dr. Alberto Cervantes and Jesus Carmona proudly show off Lluvia's first multiple litter. Though the tigress accepted all three of her cubs, she would gladly surrender them to Carmona while she took a short break in an adjoining cage.

Alberto Cervantes was born the oldest of four children in Tepic, Nayarit. His father worked at a gas station and his mother was a housewife. When he was growing up, Alberto had a passion for wildlife and loved watching Animal Planet and the Discovery Channel. His uncle worked with turtles in San Blas, Nayarit, and invited young Alberto to join him in his study of turtles and crocodiles.

At the age of fifteen, Cervantes decided to become a veterinarian and began college in 1998 at the Universidad Autonoma de Nayarit. He

expected to treat deer, goats, dogs, cats, and of course, crocodiles and turtles.

In 2004, Dr. Calderon brought Cervantes to Paradise Village so he could write his thesis based on the animals there. "I remember seeing the tigers up close for the first time. Then, during the six months I worked on my thesis, I saw how Jesus Carmona treated and cared for the baby tigers: like they were members of his family. He even calls them his kids. I said to myself, 'I would love to do just that.'"

Cervantes now spends his spare time reading books about tigers, going to conferences on felines, studying videos, and learning from Carmona. He has a childlike excitement that disguises his age and years of study. "I love everything about the tigers. I have a lot of respect and love for them. I like to be around them and see how noble and intelligent they are. I learn from them every single day."

When asked if he felt he was in danger when working with the tigers, he answers quickly, "Never." Then he adds, "Well…maybe with Chloe. She had a temper, but it was never anything really serious."

Cervantes identifies the most difficult part of his job as feeling helpless when he can't find the solution to make a tiger feel better. One heart-breaking example was a cub that was rejected at birth and diagnosed with kidney failure. For two months Cervantes, Carmona, and Mary worked tirelessly to save its life. In the end, it would have needed complete blood replacement, which was impossible. Despite all their efforts, the cub died. Losses like this stay with Cervantes. He spends hours rethinking strategies that didn't work and trying to improve treatment for the next cub.

If he had to anything to tell the Paradise Village visitors; it would be, "The tigers here are really well cared for. They have a full-time doctor, a full-time zookeeper, and with the support and supervision of Mr. Sovernigo and Mr. Carmona, we are helping to preserve these beautiful creatures."

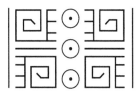

Juan Diaz

Head zookeeper Juan Diaz had been with Paradise Village longer than the tigers. He and his staff took care of all the cages at the hotel, El Tigre, and the zoo. The hours were long and the work was tough, but Juan is tougher.

Diaz was born in Telolapan, Guerrero, which is near Acapulco. When he was finally able to escape the poverty and crime of his home town, he moved to Nuevo Vallarta and got a job at Paradise Village as a gardener in 1994.

One of his duties was to clean the cages of the first animals living at the resort. This job started simply enough with three deer, but soon came rabbits, peacocks, ostriches, raccoons, crocodiles, and finally tigers.

Diaz was quickly moved from the landscaping staff to full-time zookeeper, in charge of cleaning all the cages and feeding and caring for all the animals. He was there the day Leoncio arrived. "It was the first time in my life that I saw a tiger. I jumped at the opportunity to get closer and pet him."

When I first met Diaz, he was escorting three-month-old Samantha around the grounds. Not only was he allowing people to encounter their first tiger, he was allowing Samantha the chance to become acquainted with humans. He watched her carefully and told everyone how and where to pet her. At that time, he spoke no English, but the way he treated Samantha provided a model for the rest of us.

His love for the tigers is seen in his eyes when he recalls Leoncio's death. "It was very sad. He couldn't move or walk. In twenty-four hours he was gone."

A normal workday for the crew begins early in the morning as they clean the animal cages at the hotel, El Tigre, and the zoo. When it comes to the tigers, they make sure their cages and pools are clean, and their waterfalls are in working order. First the tigers are moved to their den boxes or holding areas, so workers can enter the cages. Grassy areas are raked and inspected for signs of bleeding, breeding, or illness. Any uneaten food from the night before is picked up and thrown away so

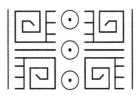

Head Zookeeper Juan Diaz.

the tigers won't get sick. The den boxes and concrete areas are hosed down, and if the temperatures are high the tigers are washed with the hose, while keeping the spray away from their faces.

Diaz said the toughest part of his day was just getting the tigers to move to their holding areas so he could clean the cages. Spraying a defiant tiger in the face with a water hose will get it to move into its holding cage, but Diaz hated to do that. "Sometimes, they're not in a

good mood and they don't want to move. So I just get my stuff and move on. I don't take chances. Eventually the tigers cooperate."

At feeding time, each tiger has different requirements when it comes to how much and what kind of food it gets. In some instances, nutritional supplements and medications are concealed in the food that is placed in the den boxes.

In all his years with the Bengal program, Diaz has been injured by a tiger only once. A few years ago, Lluvia was particularly agitated and overly protective of her cubs. Diaz was outside the cage, raking between the cage bars and the safety fence. When he took his eyes off Lluvia for a moment, the tigress reached through the bars and hit him in the head with her paw. "I felt like a professional boxer hit me." Diaz ended up with a concussion and a broken nose. "Never take your eyes off a tiger."

Even with that injury, Diaz said he never felt he was in danger when working with the tigers. "They've all grown up here. We know them; they know us. But they're wild animals and very, very strong. I respect their power."

He still recalls the night Nala fought Khan. "We thought she was dead. It took her eight months to recover. It was frightening to see how much damage Khan did in just one minute."

He says that many people ask him about the man who reaches inside the cages to hug and kiss the adult tigers. "I tell them, 'That's Mr. Carmona; he is their father. He oversees the Bengal program and he knows them better than anyone.' When they ask me why I don't do that, I tell them, 'Because I'm not crazy.'"

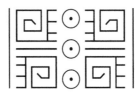

A Mate For Leoncio:
Finding Casimira

Paradise Village had been very successful nursing Leoncio back to health and giving him a good life. Don Graziano, Carmona, and Dr. Gonzalo Calderon discussed the possibility of getting a mate for the little male tiger.

Coincidently, the veterinarian in Guadalajara called Don Graziano. He knew of Leoncio's recovery and had another challenge for Paradise Village: a little female. She was very sick, but maybe Don Graziano's staff could help this tiger, too.

When the female cub arrived, Carmona's heart sank. The cub was close to death. Don Graziano spared no expense getting her the best and most advanced care he could give her. Carmona, Dr. Calderon, and the zoo staff worked around the clock to make her well.

In spite of all their efforts the female died after three months. The veterinarian in Guadalajara was notified and he requested the female be returned to his office so he could perform an autopsy, in hopes they would all better understand what had happened. She was immediately transported back.

Leoncio, who had never even gotten to share a cage with her, was still without a mate. He was two years old before another female was found for him. She was beautiful, healthy, and her name was Casimira. She and Leoncio made a perfect breeding pair and began the Paradise Village Bengal family tree.

Casimira, Paradise Village's second tiger and matriarch of the tiger program.

The First Cubs Arrive
in Paradise Village

Casimira's second litter.

After sharing a cage for a year, Casimira gave birth to her first cubs: three females and one male. Carmona and Don Graziano were jubilant that all four were healthy. But they hadn't counted on Casimira rejecting the entire litter.

A tigress's first litter is often rejected for a couple reasons. One of them might be the tigress's confusion at this new experience; another could be hormone imbalances that occur. No matter what the cause, Casimira wanted nothing to do with her cubs.

Carmona helps transition young Chloe by visiting her inside her new cage.
Soon, he would greet her only through the cage bars.

Calls were made to zoos in the U.S. and Mexico to ask for advice.
Soon the cubs were relocated to Carmona's house, where he was joined
by staff members and volunteers to help raise them.

Even though the new arrangements were chaotic, Carmona
knew this would be the beginning of something special, something
unique. Don Graziano funded the building of more habitats, more zoo
personnel were hired, and the cubs enjoyed Carmona's house until their
new homes were completed.

Carmona, with the help of employees from housekeeping and other departments, cared for the litter. He played with them, fed them, and napped with them. He knew a day would come when they would have to leave his home and go to cages, but he pushed the thought away until it finally became a reality.

The separation was—and always is—heartbreaking. Carmona and Mary do what they can to make a young tiger's transition to life in a cage as easy as possible. At first, cage time would be kept to a few hours a day. When the tigers were ready to spend the whole night in a cage, the Carmonas would bring sleeping bags and camp out with them. Eventually the visits were shortened. The process could take weeks, but Carmona admits that it eased his aching heart, too.

Carmona made daily visits to the cages to see his kids, and they loved seeing him.

Cats in *The Jungle*

Junior, eight weeks old, spends the morning resting on the cool floor in Carmona's office.

In 2000, the Paradise Village Mall saw the opening of a new restaurant/night club. Don Graziano and Carmona had envisioned a restaurant that would be a cross between a Hard Rock Café and a Rainforest Café. Since the Paradise Village Zoo had begun to grow in size and popularity, they decided to call the restaurant The Jungle.

Carmona juggled his time between developing The Jungle and overseeing the tiger program. One of the duties in raising wild animals is to make them *tractable*. No Paradise Village tiger is tame, but it will

grow up familiar with human scent and be at ease as humans pass by its cage. At El Tigre Golf Course, or at the resort, you might have seen a tiger cub being walked on a leash. That is all part of the cub's socialization. All of Leoncio and Casimira's cubs were socialized in this manner.

With the opening of The Jungle, Carmona realized he had a chance to socialize cubs and create a novel atmosphere in the restaurant. He would walk a cub through the restaurant so the patrons could see it. As you can guess, the nightly tiger walk through The Jungle was the highlight of the diners' experience.

The first cub, Junior, really enjoyed the job and seemed to love the attention from humans. Carmona would complain to customers that the new night manager was lazy and didn't know what he was doing. Then, to everyone's surprise, he'd bring in Junior as the new night manager.

During the day, Carmona ran an educational tiger encounter with children and teens. He especially liked including teens because they were deciding on career paths. They would sit in a circle and Junior would wander among them while Carmona explained the lives of tigers and the realities of extinction. Some of the children who were a part of these early encounters have returned to Paradise Village to thank Carmona. Because of his inspiration and Junior's willingness to interact with them, many of these teens have grown up to become veterinarians, zookeepers, or ecologists.

At five months old, Junior was transferred to a zoo. But other tiger cubs would follow in his…paw prints. 🐾

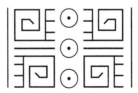

Tiger Saves Man's Life

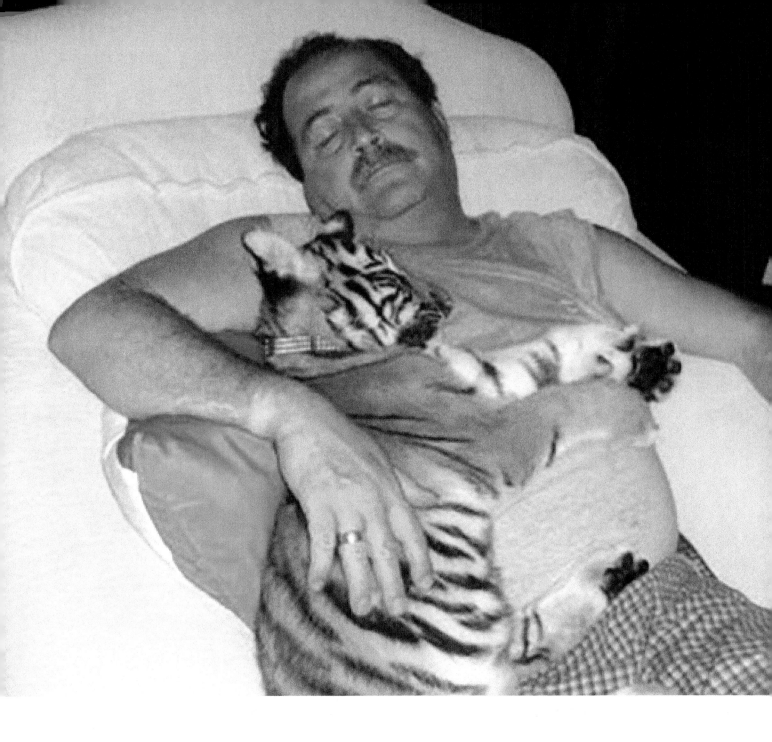

Carmona and three-month-old Diego enjoyed afternoon naps.

Carmona was developing The Jungle while still grieving the sudden death of his wife. Death had touched his life very few times, and no loss had been as devastatingly painful as this one. His friends worried that he would crawl in a bottle and stay there. Even he didn't feel he had any other option.

Until Diego arrived.

Casimira and Leoncio had produced an extraordinary litter. Generally, tigers give birth to two or three cubs, four at the most. This

46

is because tiger cubs are virtually helpless when born. They cannot see for two to three weeks, and stagger unsteadily for about a month. In the wild, caring for a larger litter would be next to impossible for a tigress.

Casimira had given birth to five cubs.

She immediately chose the four cubs she would nurture and the one she would reject: a little male. She allowed the rest of her litter to nurse, but pushed away the fifth cub. Rejection in this case was a long-ago instinct from the wild; it was more important to raise four, strong, healthy cubs than five weaker ones.

Carmona watched the rejected male struggle for Casimira's attention and developed a kinship with this lost cub. He would have to remove the cub from the litter in order to save its life. More importantly he would have to hand-raise the cub if it were to have a chance at survival.

In that instant, Carmona found purpose. He had read books and learned what he could from zookeepers, but now he would dedicate his efforts to becoming an expert on tiger behavior. He would spend all of his time with this little cub and maybe through the circumstances of their losses they could forge a unique bond between human and animal.

From that day forward, the tiger cub named Diego became Carmona's reason for living.

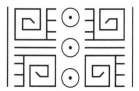

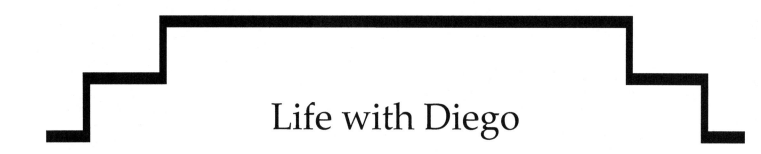

Life with Diego

Carmona and five-month-old Diego were inseparable.

Most people think it would be great to have a baby tiger in the house. Answering your door and nonchalantly talking to the mailman while a tiger cub snakes between your legs seems like a great way to make an impression. But tigers, like other exotic felines, are no picnic to raise.

The first responsibility is proper nutrition. Cubs that stay with their mothers get all the nutrients they need from mother's milk. However, when a cub has been rejected, humans have to intervene

and bottle feed the rejected baby. Hand-raised cubs are fed a formula that is a combination of several ingredients designed to meet their nutritional needs. Tigers have a large amount of muscle mass that develops very quickly in the first year. This requires protein that can be quickly broken down by the newborn's digestive system. For that reason, the formula base is a powdered kitten formula available through U.S. veterinarians. When mixed with warm water, it provides easily digestible protein. Secondly, there is a special, calcium-rich powdered supplement to aid in the rapid growth of a tiger's dense, heavy bones. The final ingredients include an array of vitamins, minerals, enzymes, and amino acids, which are all present in a tiger-mother's milk.

That takes care of what to feed a baby tiger. The second challenge is when. Since tiger cubs free-feed from their mothers for months, usually nursing every two to three hours, a hand-raised cub needs a freshly mixed bottle of formula for every feeding. Don't worry. He'll let you know when he's hungry. His scream is loud and insistent and doesn't stop until the bottle is in his mouth. The Carmonas have gotten phone calls from neighbors wanting to know if they were taking care of a human baby.

When the cubs are two to three months old, the tigress will begin introducing meat to her young by chewing it up and spitting it out for the cubs to eat. This food is in addition to the mother's milk they still receive. The hand-raised cub also needs fresh meat, pulverized into a blob and placed on the floor in front of him. A tiger-raised cub has seen and smelled raw meat when his mother eats it. A human-raised cub will often stare at the meat, then back away and demand more formula instead. Carmona admits that there have been times when he's put the ground meat in his mouth, then spit it out for the cub. Apparently that sends the proper message.

The next job in hand-raising is bathroom duty. After a cub is done feeding, the tigress licks the cub's rear end to stimulate the bowels and bladder. She continues doing this until the cub successfully eliminates

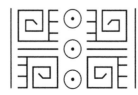

waste. With a hand-raised cub, the human parent must end each feeding session stroking the cub's rear end with a rough washcloth to simulate its mother's tongue. This is done until the cub has a successful elimination. Mop duty and loads of laundry are the result.

A human baby can be bottle fed, burped, and put back to sleep, but a tiger cub demands thirty to forty-five minutes of constant attention at feeding time. This doesn't allow much time for sleep…or anything else.

This was the schedule Carmona faced as the single parent of a tiger cub. With the development of El Tigre Golf Course and the Hacienda Country Club, Carmona's job demanded a great deal of his time and attention. The only way to report for work each day and hand-raise Diego was to take the cub to the office with him. Everyday business was conducted while Carmona bottle-fed Diego. As the cub grew older, he loved riding shotgun in Carmona's sports car, or making the rounds as a passenger in Carmona's golf cart. At six and seven months old, Diego would sleep peacefully under Carmona's desk while interviews, negotiations, and phone calls went on overhead. Usually, the people involved in the meetings didn't know that a tiger slept beneath the desk. It was only when Diego woke up and interrupted the conversation with a groaning yawn that guests would become curious. Carmona recalls, "I would tell people not to worry. It was just my tiger." Meetings usually ended pretty quickly after that.

While Carmona had studied tigers for some time, he felt he got his real education during his months with Diego. He felt fortunate that Diego was a mellow guy. No big mood swings, no challenges for power. As tigers go, Diego was easy to read. And he loved nothing better than to be with his human dad every minute of every day.

Because tigers in the wild lead solitary lives, they're generally quiet animals. They stay hidden and rarely roar or attract attention to themselves. However, Diego was always pretty vocal in his affection for Carmona, communicating with a vocabulary of *chuffs* and groans.

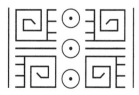

It's possible that hearing human dialogue at home and in Carmona's office made Diego more talkative.

At one year old, Diego weighed 170 pounds and measured four feet from his nose to the tip of his tail. Still there was no cage in his reality. His days were filled with golf cart rides and naps under the desk. He eagerly drank in every second of his daily rides in Carmona's car. At night, Diego and Carmona shared a condo like two easygoing bachelors…two mellow guys.

Of course, Carmona delighted in Diego's antics and endured the daily destruction of lamps, rugs, and collectibles. Leaving Diego alone in the house was never an option. A tiger—especially Diego—could get into mischief in the blink of an eye. In fact, one afternoon as Carmona took a half hour nap in the bedroom, Diego tore apart the living room sofa. There was nothing left but splinters, stuffing, and scraps of upholstery.

Whether he liked it or not, Carmona had to face reality. Diego could no longer be allowed to roam free in the house. Carmona's tiger roommate had never shown any sign of aggression or challenge for dominance, but like all wild animals Diego had grown big and strong, with no concept of his physical power. At a year old, a single swat from a tiger's paw can cause a concussion. A playful ambush could break Carmona's back, or worse, kill him.

Though it broke his heart to admit it, it was time for Carmona to put Diego in a cage.

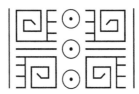

Diego and the Great Escape(s)

Diego "riding shotgun" in Carmona's golf cart.

Carmona couldn't bear to have Diego in a cage at the hotel. It was too far away. Besides, El Tigre Golf Course was the only place Diego knew other than his home in the condo. Carmona wanted to make the transition to a cage as easy for Diego as possible.

Don Graziano agreed to build a cage outside the pro shop. This would allow Diego to be in a familiar place with the stimulation of people going in and out of the shop all day. It was reasoned that by night, Diego would be tired and fall into an exhausted sleep in his new

cage. During Diego's first day in the golf course cage, Carmona spent a lot of time with him. The day was bittersweet with Carmona realizing that he would miss Diego's company when it was time to go home. At the end of the day, Carmona said goodbye to Diego, got in his sports car, and drove away to face his empty, quiet, tiger-less condo.

Night came, and with it a phone call: the security guards at El Tigre had found Diego's cage empty. Panic and guilt gripped Carmona as he ran to his sports car and drove to the golf course. In all his time as the director of the tiger program, no tiger had ever escaped. And now Diego—his mellow guy, his best friend, his roommate—was gone. He pulled up next to Diego's cage and jumped out of the car. He left the car's headlights shining onto the darkened driving range as he and the guards formed their search party strategy. Armed with flashlights, a leather collar and thick rope, the men headed into the darkness. The hunt for Diego was on.

Carmona headed across the driving range and into the trees calling Diego's name, then stopping to listen. Questions raced through his head. Was Diego hurt? Was he stalking through the trees? "Diego! I'm here! Come out, Handsome!" Carmona's ears strained to hear footsteps, movement of any kind. He called out again. This time when he stopped to listen, he heard Diego groan. He ran toward the voice, shouting Diego's name again. Diego replied with another, longer moan. By now Carmona was making his way out of the trees and onto the driving range. He called to Diego again; the tiger responded. This call-and-response continued as Carmona ran up the slope to the pro shop. That's when Carmona saw Diego, sitting in the passenger seat of Carmona's sports car, riding shotgun, ready to go home.

And home is where they went. Back to the condo.

It was determined that the spaces between the cage bars were just a little too wide and Diego's desperation to escape had been too great. He had managed to squeeze through two of the vertical bars in his effort to find Carmona. Diego wasn't ready—and wasn't large enough—to stay overnight in the pro shop cage. However, it was decided that Diego

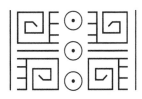

55

would go into the cage during the day. He liked all the attention and responded happily to all the people who stopped by to talk to him.

There was only one problem. Once Diego found he *could* escape, he decided he *would* escape.

The next episode was during a sudden thunderstorm. Carmona was radioed that Diego had escaped. He raced through the downpour to the cage in back of the pro shop. There he found Diego leaning up against the pro shop door trying to keep dry under the eaves while a dozen wide-eyed adults stood on the other side of the door. It was then decided not to keep Diego in the pro shop cage if there was a threat of rain.

Carmona kept him at home for awhile knowing he'd quickly grow too big to escape. Once again Diego rode to work with Carmona on a peaceful, sunny morning. The golf course was busy that day. A steady stream of carts made their way to the tees, and golfers lined up at the driving range to practice their swings. Maybe it was so busy that no one was paying attention to Diego.

So he left.

No one saw him squeeze through the bars, but he did it again. Diego managed to get all the way to the stand of trees past the driving range without being detected. It was only when he decided he'd done enough wandering and was strolling happily across the driving range toward the pro shop that everyone noticed. There was a terrified shout, "Tiger!"

Golfers threw down their clubs and scattered in every direction. It is said that within thirty seconds not a single golfer was in sight. The staff radioed Carmona and he came running. Diego was happy to see him and ready to go back into his cage.

Unfortunately for Diego, he finally reached a size that made escape impossible. Clearing the driving range of every golfer and groundskeeper was the last performance of Diego, the Great Escape Artist.

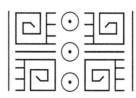

The Carmonas' Scrapbook
Babes in Paradise

The Arrival of Khan

In 2003, as Samantha approached breeding age, it was now time to look for a suitable mate outside of the Paradise Village gene pool. After a couple months of paperwork, government permits, and shipping agreements between facilities, Guadalajara Zoo was ready to transport their male cub.

In December, four-month-old Khan arrived at Paradise Village at 1:30 in the morning. Carmona and Dr. Calderon were waiting for him in the parking garage. The cub had suffered from severe motion sickness during his trip and had vomited all over himself and his cage. He was weak, hungry, and very agitated.

Dr. Calderon looked him over without taking him out of the cage and concluded that the cub was doing as well as could be expected after the long trip. Tomorrow they would examine him more closely.

Carmona stayed with Khan to calm him down. He spoke softly to the cub, then pushed a piece of raw chicken through the cage bars to lure Khan to one corner. While the cub ate, Carmona got a water hose and with gentle pressure began washing the bottom of the cage. When that was clean, he led the cub to another corner and washed the rest of the cage floor.

As the cub calmed down, Carmona ran the water over Kahn's feet and legs. Pretty soon, Carmona had his hand in the cage rubbing Khan's bristling fur and washing the cub's body.

With a clean cage, clean fur, and a belly full of chicken, Khan settled down to rest. Carmona headed for home to get some sleep. As he reached the garage exit, he heard a terrible scream. It came from the transport cage and echoed through the concrete garage. He ran back to see what was the matter.

When Khan saw Carmona, he quietly settled back down to rest. Khan wanted Carmona to stay with him. That was the beginning of a long night in the parking garage with a scared little tiger cub.

By the next day, Carmona was walking Khan on a leash and the little cub was devoted to his new friend. Khan went everywhere with Carmona except in the car. You see, Diego was still living at home with Carmona and loved riding in the car. Khan took one sniff of Carmona's

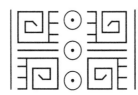

Samantha proved to be a very patient and loving mother, rejecting very few cubs.

car and decided it was somebody else's territory. Somebody bigger and older. So Kahn refused to ride in the car.

Eventually the sweet, playful cub was residing at the hotel in the cage next to Samantha. When the two shared the same cage, he acted like a big goofball and she acted like a babysitter who wished the kid's parents would come home. As he grew older and both reached breeding age they became strong, regal breeding partners.

With over five hundred pounds of dense muscle and heavy bone,
Khan spends much of the day cooling off in his pool.

To this day, Khan is in love with the water. While all tigers like to
cool off in water, for Khan it's a huge part of his daily to-do list.

I wonder if it has something to do with that first night in the
parking garage when chicken, soft words, and gently flowing water
restored his health and psyche. 🐾

The Science of Extinction

Most of us have seen pictures of dinosaurs and have pondered the extinction of a species. There are many contributing factors to extinction: lack of habitat and over-hunting are the two principal reasons a species enters the endangered list. But when does an animal become extinct? I used to have a Noah's Ark view of extinction; as long as we had one male and one female, we had hope.

While volunteering at the Exotic Feline Breeding Compound in Rosamond, California, I learned the awful truth about extinction. Hope is gone much earlier than that.

The science part of extinction comes down to genetics. Darwin called it natural selection. When the strongest male who has successfully adapted to his environment mates with the strongest female, the genes which govern those strengths are passed to the offspring. When a species has lots of possible mates, genes that are responsible for weaker traits have less chance of being expressed through the offspring.

In the 1950s, blonde Cocker Spaniels became an overnight sensation. In order to supply the demand for all those puppies, many irresponsible dog owners cashed in on the craze by inbreeding their dogs: mothers to sons, fathers to daughters, and brothers to sisters. Every breed has genetic traits that are considered weaknesses. When you breed two dogs with exactly the same weaknesses, you get weak dogs. Many of the blonde Cocker Spaniels bred during that time lived only a short while. Many displayed a nasty and unpredictable temperament that resulted in them being abandoned or euthanized. Every time a breed of dog enjoys overnight popularity, reputable breeders are disheartened. They know unscrupulous breeders will turn out thousands of poorly-bred, weak, sickly, ill-tempered, inbred dogs as a result of a narrow gene pool.

We humans used to have a group of people whose inbreeding led to disease, physical deformities, and insanity: nobility. Centuries ago, when marriages were arranged among nobles, marrying within the family kept a noble's landholdings safe. Unfortunately the gene pool

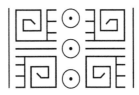

was too narrow and genetic weaknesses emerged. Henry VIII's first daughter, Mary, was wed to a prince who was four feet tall, drooled uncontrollably, picked at his skin with a knife, and slept on a block of ice. By the way, poor Mary wasn't much of a bargain herself. Luckily, the gene pool for nobles is much better managed these days.

In the case of the blond Cocker Spaniels, as with the nobles of history, the culprit was a narrow gene pool. The same culprit is the reason for extinction of a species. When there are fewer animals, there is a greater chance of inbreeding.

If an area supports forty tigers, all from the same family tree, the chance of inbred weakness increases. As those offspring breed with each other, the number of weak offspring grows. Eventually, while there may be a few hundred of a species left, all the litters will produce cubs that are stillborn or die soon after birth. Extinction doesn't come when the last male and female die. It's already a fact when hundreds are left.

The Paradise Village Bengal Tiger Program seeks to keep the Bengal gene pool wide. Lineage of each tiger is considered before a breeding pair is put together. The cubs bred here are transported to zoos and compounds to enhance their gene pools. Khan and Daisy were brought to Paradise Village so the gene pool could stay strong. Exchange and/or transport of tigers never involves a sale; this is not about profit. The practice, as it is with most zoos and compounds in the U.S., is to negotiate transportation expenses between the two participating organizations. The only concern is the preservation of the Bengal tiger gene pool. 🐾

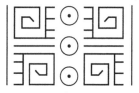

Zookeeper Down!

Former landscaper Juan Diaz, who had become Dr. Calderon's assistant, worked alongside the veterinarian to get the Bengal program up and running. Since taking care of Bengal tigers was new to both men, there were some disagreements between Calderon and Diaz. Diaz had the practical experience of being with the animals everyday; Calderon had intellectual knowledge and theory from the books he read.

One time, the zoo's crocodile had clamped his mouth around a parrot that had flown into its cage. Visitors were horrified and yelled for help. Though there was nothing to be done for the poor parrot, they had to try, if only to appease the crowd. Calderon ordered Diaz to enter the cage, jump on the crocodile's back, and hold its mouth closed until Calderon could throw a noose over the croc's snout. It seemed to Diaz that Dr. Calderon wasn't very interested in Diaz's safety, so he suggested Calderon jump on the croc's back and Diaz would lasso it. The ensuing argument did nothing to help the parrot or subdue the crocodile.

However, the major disagreement between Diaz and Calderon involved a gun that shot tranquilizing darts. Diaz had discovered that a tiger was sick and needed immediate care. He quickly called for Calderon to come to the cage. Calderon brought his brand new dart gun so they could tranquilize the animal and get into the cage for treatment.

Diaz had been observing the animal from one side of the cage, and Calderon joined him, loading his dart gun. After analyzing his position, Calderon didn't feel he had a good shot, so he slowly walked to another section of cage bars. He took aim and fired. The dart sailed over the animal and into Diaz's thigh. Diaz howled and pulled the dart out. The tranquilizer in the dart wasn't a factor in the injury; it was the speed of the dart. Tranquilizing guns shoot with enough power to pierce an animal's tough hide and sink deep into the muscle. Calderon's dart had gone through Diaz's muscle and lodged in the bone.

Calderon was shaken and concerned for Diaz, but Diaz pulled out the dart and shouted for Calderon to take another shot; they had to help

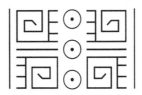

71

the tiger. Calderon loaded the dart gun and both men changed their positions. Calderon fired a second time…and hit Diaz again: this time in the arm.

People who were there say a string of obscenities poured out of Diaz's mouth as he pulled the second dart out of the bone in his upper arm and finally left to get medical care. Diaz had a healthy mistrust of Calderon's capabilities as a marksman after that incident. 🐾

Mary Meets Nala

Nala, like Faith (above) looked forward to her short rides in the *Critter Car.*

Mary had met Carmona in Puerto Vallarta at his restaurant. Whenever she came to town, she would stop by to see him. When Carmona left for Paradise Village, he kept up correspondence with her. Upon hearing that she would be visiting Puerto Vallarta again, he invited her to see all the new developments at Paradise Village.

When Carmona picked her up, she was surprised to find a three-month-old tiger in the back seat. Mary kept an eye on the tiger hoping it wouldn't attack her. Before they had a chance to see the grounds,

Carmona pulled up to an office at the resort and got out of the car, promising he'd be "just a minute." To Mary's shock, she realized that Carmona planned to leave the tiger with her.

"Hey! Wait!" she shouted after him. "There's a tiger in here. What if she starts acting crazy?"

Carmona looked in the back. Nala was sleeping peacefully and probably would continue to do so. He reached down under the front seat and pulled out an old, crooked stick. "Here," he said as he handed it to her. "If she acts crazy, just show her the stick. I'll only be gone a minute." And with that he disappeared into the building.

People have heard of the Hawaiian Minute or the Mexican Minute. But the Carmona Minute can take an hour. Taking a look at the sleeping tiger, she began to question herself. Do I trust this man enough to do this? She glanced at the door where Carmona had entered. Do I like this man enough to stay in the car with a tiger and a stick? She studied the stick, then look over her shoulder at Nala. The answer—finally—was yes.

Mary endured the Carmona minute and her first experience with a tiger by looking over her shoulder every couple minutes. If Nala stretched or yawned, Mary held the stick up. When Nala went back to sleep, Mary put the stick down. Mary laughs, "One time the poor baby kind of blinked…Stick up!"

That was a few years ago. Since then, Mary has learned that when you get to know a tiger, you create a mutual respect for one another. "They know how far to push you, and you know what to expect."

When Carmona and Mary wed, Carmona found homes for the seven cats he had rescued and began teaching Mary how to raise tigers. 🐾

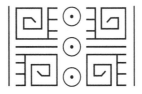

Living La Vida El Tigre

Lluvia is "The Face of El Tigre Golf Course" thanks to her beautiful facial markings.

Seasoned guests of Paradise Village may remember Samantha's walks beside the hotel pools, Nala's get-acquainted visits by the Palenque Spa, or Diego's visits to the lobby of the Tikal Tower. In the early days, it seemed easier for guests to have a tiger cub encounter.

That's because it was.

Paradise Village has all the permits and legal documents to keep tigers as long as they stay on the resort property. Samantha, Nala, and

Diego grew up at the zoo cages in front of the Uxmal Tower. It was easy for Diaz to take a cub out of the cage and walk it around.

Once El Tigre Golf Course was built, cubs were no longer raised in the cages at the hotel. El Tigre had larger habitats on the far end of the golf course, but that posed a logistics problem for the old-fashioned tiger encounters. The cubs are permitted to walk, ride in golf carts or cars on Paradise Village property only. A cub that is raised on the golf course needs to be transported across public land to get to the resort. That takes a different kind of permit and is much harder to obtain.

Three people held permits to transport tigers across public land: Don Graziano, Carmona, and the vet...three of the busiest men around. So tiger cubs rarely got the opportunity to visit the hotel and walk around the pools. If you wanted to see them, you had to visit the cages at the far end of the golf course.

Lluvia's Kodak Moment

Mary Carmona's first interaction with a tiger older than three months, was with Lluvia. Lluvia, the last cub of Casimira and Leoncio, had lived in Carmona's house until she was eight months old. Unlike Diego, who was a mellow guy, Lluvia had an independent streak that made her cage-ready at eight months. Carmona made a point to play with her in her cage everyday to help her adjust to her new habitat.

One day, when Mary was visiting, Carmona decided to take her to Lluvia's cage. Lluvia was delighted to see him. She greeted him with chuffs and pushed the side of her face against his hand when he reached inside the cage. Mary was won over instantly by the affection Lluvia showed for her Carmona.

Carmona then entered the cage to play with Lluvia, leaving Mary between the cage bars and the safety fence. The eight-month-old circled him repeatedly. Mary, ever the photographer, realized she had a genuine Kodak moment in the making. How many people get the chance to photograph a tiger without cage bars or chain link fences in the way? She fumbled for her camera, while Carmona played with Lluvia.

Inside the cage, Carmona spotted one of Lluvia's favorite toys. He made the mistake of turning his back on the tigress to pick up the toy. When he turned around he was greeted by 150 pounds of tiger leaping on him, putting paws on his shoulders, and licking his neck. Mary laughed, stuck her camera through the cage bars, and began taking pictures. "Oh, that's so cute!" she shouted.

Carmona dropped the toy and fought to keep his balance. As he staggered for a better footing, he talked lovingly to Lluvia. He did his best to appear calm, but he was struggling under the burden of the tiger's weight. Mary protested, "No, no! Stay there! I want to get some more pictures!"

Getting out from under Lluvia's big paws was no easy task, but he finally managed. As he joined Mary outside the cage, he hoped she got the shot she wanted because he wasn't going to put himself in that predicament again. 🐾

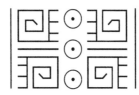

Lluvia Meets "Daddy's New Girlfriend"

Mary accompanied Carmona every day to eight-month-old Lluvia's cage. Tucked between the safety fence and the cage bars, she took pictures and watched Carmona hug Lluvia and play with her.

Eventually, Carmona decided to formally introduce Mary to Lluvia. His plan was to lead Lluvia over to the cage bars so the two could get acquainted. Mary was excited about the prospect of being up-close-and-personal with the tiger, but she hadn't been given any of the details concerning the introduction. Carmona stepped inside the cage, telling Mary, "Be sure the door is shut."

Mary assumed the introduction was going to take place in the cage, so she stepped inside, shut the door behind her, and followed Carmona. Lluvia saw the intruder and trotted past him. Carmona looked behind him and was horrified to see Mary in the cage. Out of all the tigers he had raised, Lluvia was the most possessive and territorial. This breech of territory had the potential for real disaster. He lightly grabbed Lluvia's tail and held on, hoping to slow the tiger down. It didn't work. Lluvia had caught the scent of Carmona on this new female and she wasn't pleased. She nipped at Mary.

Carmona held Lluvia's tail tighter, but the tiger nipped again. Mary, stunned and motionless, looked to Carmona for help.

Carmona, who literally had a tiger by the tail, yelled to Mary, "Get out of here! Now!"

Mary backed inside the first open door. She quickly slammed the door and heard the lock click into place. The instant Mary was out of the cage, Lluvia settled down, happy to have her daddy all to herself.

"Are you all right?" Carmona shouted to Mary. "Yeah. I'm fine," she replied.

"Well, good, because you just locked yourself into a holding cage and I don't have the key for it. It may take awhile to get you out of there."

Mary brushed herself off and sat down in the middle of her cage.

"I don't care if it takes two or three days. I'm here, she's there. I'm happy." 🐾

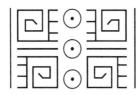

A Tragic Mistake is Made

Carmona gives five-month-old Nala a hug during their play time.

Zoos, compounds, and no-kill shelters for every type of animal are in the business of preserving life. But they will all acknowledge that mistakes are made: a misdiagnosis of a medical problem, an error in judgment about a breeding choice, misinformation about an animal that needs special care. When your mission is to save lives, losing an animal due to human error is devastating.

Casimira, the mother of Diego, Samantha, Nala, Lluvia, and many other cubs, was sterilized after Lluvia's birth. She continued to share

a cage with her breeding partner, Leoncio, until his death. After that, she became fiercely territorial and agitated with the close proximity of humans and animals at the resort. Carmona had her moved to a single cage at one end of the golf course where she could enjoy solitude. However, she soon seemed to miss the stimulation she had at Paradise Village. All the tiger cages were filled, so there were no other options at that time.

A zoo in Sinaloa was completing paperwork to take Nala. She had refused Khan, who had almost killed her, so she needed to be placed somewhere with a genetically suitable breeding partner…and this one had available young males waiting. When zoo officials learned about Casimira, they offered to take her in addition to Nala, since their tiger program was young and Casimira was a beautiful, full-grown tigress. They knew she was retired from breeding, and they agreed to Carmona's only demand: she was an extremely territorial female who must be caged by herself.

The zoo environment gave Casimira the stimulation of visitors but from a greater distance. In her new location, she thrived and appeared to be accepting of the other tigers around her. Zoo employees, needing to repair another cage, misread Casimira's docile behavior and temporarily relocated another female into her cage. The old territorial streak rose with a vengeance and Casimira attacked. The result was a fight to the death. Casimira died at the fangs of a younger tigress in September of 2007. That younger female was her daughter, Nala.

The workers at the zoo knew Nala was Casimira's daughter, but didn't know Nala had been rejected at birth. They assumed mother and daughter would be fine during the temporary relocation. But when a tigress rejects a cub, that offspring is never welcomed back.

The humans who work with the tigers at Paradise Village were dumbstruck. They had done everything they could to give Casimira a peaceful life, and now she was dead. And Nala, who had almost been killed by Khan, had been traumatized a second time when she was forced to fight for her life again.

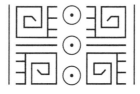

Zoos and compounds don't want to publicize that mistakes are made, but mistakes happen. This particular zoo is known thoughout Mexico for its beauty and care of its animals. Over the years it has become home to several Paradise Village cubs, offering an excellent opportunity to widen the gene pool by providing healthy breeding partners. While nothing can be done to bring back Casimira, it is important to state that Nala recovered from her injuries, found a suitable mate, and is now content and thriving. 🐾

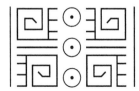

Daisy, the Sweetheart of Paradise

The search for a genetically acceptable mate for Diego moved forward. A private owner responded. The cub arrived with a long, unpronounceable Mayan name that was quickly changed to Daisy.

Daisy brought something new to the Paradise Village gene pool: she's half white Bengal. Instead of the standard bright orange color, her coat is the deep golden color of browned butter. With white tiger in her genetic code, her litters always had the chance that one might be white.

Many people mistakenly think that white tigers are weaker and therefore don't live as long as orange tigers. The survival rate of white tigers in the wild is lower because they can't hide as well, which affects their ability to ambush prey and avoid poachers. In captivity a white tiger lives as long as an orange one.

The thing that sets Daisy apart—besides her color—is her gentle, loving nature. During my visits with her when she was a cub, she would frolic through grass in the pro shop cage, then nestle beside me for long periods of time. Even the most docile tiger cubs can only put up with humans for so long, then they move away to find their own space. But Daisy has the temperament of a lap cat.

As she grew, she won the hearts of Carmona, Diaz, and Dr. Cervantes who all use the same word to describe her, "sweetheart." Even in adulthood, when other females begin to show signs of unpredictability, Daisy has remained sweet and even-tempered. While none of her caretakers venture into the cage of any adult tiger, they actually considered posing for a picture with Daisy. (They came to their senses.)

Before Daisy entered *oestrus* (heat), they placed her with Diego: the mellow guy paired with the mellowest female. The union has been a happy and peaceful one. If Diego had any complaint, it would be that Daisy wants to play with him, nuzzle with him, and keep him from his day-long naps.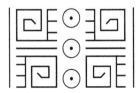

Honey-colored Daisy is half white Bengal.

The Carmonas' Scrapbook
Nap Time

Chloe is Born

Lluvia, which is Spanish for *rain*, got her name because she was born in the middle of a rainstorm. Her mother, Casimira, had been a wonderful mother to many healthy cubs that now populate many Mexican zoos. But Casimira had no desire to raise any more babies, so Lluvia was last in a series of rejections. Casimira was sterilized after Lluvia's birth, so Lluvia is the last offspring of Casimira and Leoncio.

Carmona raised Lluvia by hand until she was ready to be transferred to a cage. There she became one of two tigresses to breed with Khan. Keep in mind that in the wild, males are used to servicing two or three tigresses within their territory.

Apparently Khan was very good at his job and managed to get both tigresses pregnant within days of each other. There had been signs of breeding in Samantha's cage, but none in Lluvia's. Everyone figured Samantha was pregnant and the younger Lluvia was not.

As a severe storm system approached land, Samantha gave birth to her litter. The next night, November 1, 2007, Lluvia gave birth to her first cub, Chloe. There could be any of several reasons why Lluvia chose to actively reject the baby, but reject it she did.

Thunder pounded and the rain poured down; zookeeper Juan Diaz was on duty at Samantha's cage watching over the mother and her cubs. During almost constant flashes of lightning, Diaz looked over at Lluvia's cage and saw her come out of her den box with something in her mouth. She stood in the soaking rain and shook her head violently from side to side. Diaz had seen this behavior before; Lluvia had a cub in her mouth and was trying to kill it.

He ran to Lluvia's cage, shouting at the tiger, hoping to startle her and make her drop her cub. He turned on the hose full blast, then got on the phone to Carmona. With Khan in the cage, Diaz knew that even if Lluvia dropped the cub, the big male might finish the job. He hoped the hose would give him some control to keep Khan away from Lluvia and the baby. Carmona arrived in a matter of minutes. They opened the guillotine door and coaxed Khan into a third cage.

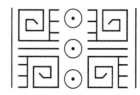

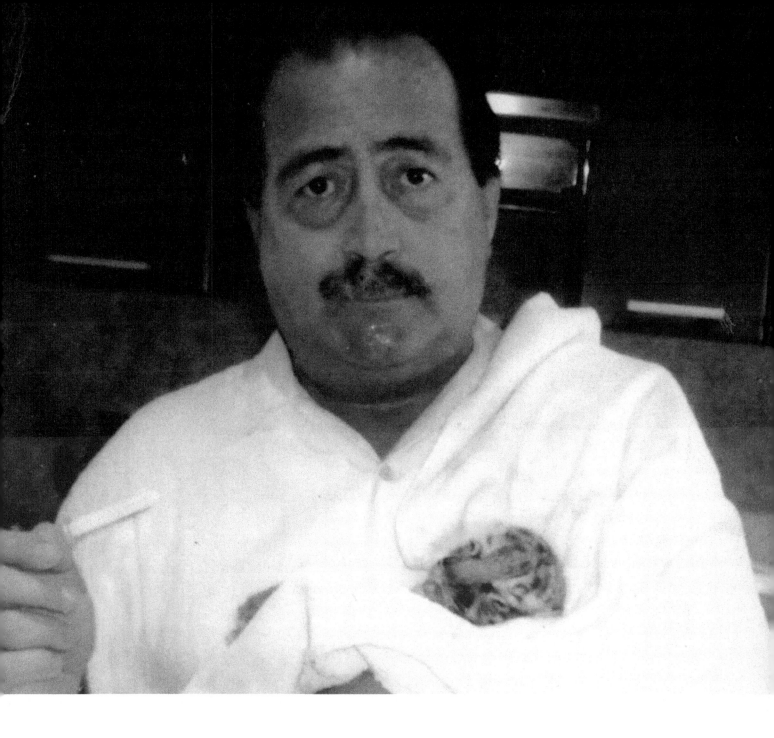

Only hours old, Chloe is fed at first with an eyedropper.

Diaz aimed the hose at Lluvia's face until she dropped the cub and backed away. Diaz kept the hose on Lluvia while Carmona entered the cage and picked up the baby.

This was Lluvia's first birthing experience, so rejection wasn't a surprise, but Carmona and the veterinarian think she also might have been confused since she'd seen Samantha's newborn cubs that day. Other theories include the birth being premature and the cub being weak. It's possible that Lluvia was killing it because she had decided

it wouldn't survive. The instincts of the wild don't take into account the development of veterinary medicine, and the increased odds that a weak cub can survive.

Within two hours of her birth, Chloe was cleaned up, wrapped in a dry towel and sleeping in Carmona's pro shop office. Unfortunately for Carmona, this was not the only drama that dark and stormy night.

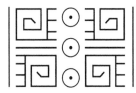

Carmona's Condo
That Same Night

"I used to be normal," Mary Carmona sighed. "I'd go to bed at ten o'clock and sleep all night."

As the tropical storm raged through Nuevo Vallarta, Mary decided to go to bed. Her husband was still awake watching television.

At three o'clock in the morning, a frantic Carmona burst into the bedroom, rifling through dresser drawers. "Mary!" he shouted. "Where's the flashlight! I need the flashlight!"

Mary sat up in bed and realized all the lights were on. "Why do you need a flashlight?"

"Just tell me where we keep the flashlight!" he shouted.

She directed him to the right drawer. He grabbed the flashlight and ran out of the room. "Don't come out! Stay in the bedroom!" He slammed the bedroom door.

Mary got out of bed, marched over to the door, flung it open and said, "You better tell me what's going on!"

She found herself face to face with Carmona and a couple of security guards. She stood defiantly in the open doorway. "Why can't I leave the room?"

Carmona answered, "Because there's a crocodile loose."

Mary stood perfectly still for a moment, then stepped back into the bedroom and shut the door.

In a classic case of it never rains but it pours—literally as well as figuratively—everything came down on Carmona's shoulders in one twenty-four hour period. The staff had been preparing for a very prestigious Canadian golf tournament. On the day before the tournament was to start, Samantha had her cubs. Then the tropical storm blew in.

During the storm, El Tigre guards got a call that a crocodile was wandering around on the golf course. Carmona was assured the guards would catch and relocate it so it wouldn't be hiding in a water hazard during the next day's golf tournament. Carmona was waiting to hear from the guards when he got the frantic call from Juan Diaz that Lluvia

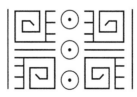

was rejecting a cub. Carmona grabbed his jacket, ran to his car, and headed for the tiger cages.

While he was gone, the guards caught the crocodile, tied a restraint around its snout and another around its front legs. They placed it on Carmona's patio, figuring he'd deal with it when he got back.

When Carmona returned home after cleaning up Chloe and fixing her a bed, he got a call about moving the crocodile. He checked the patio and the croc was gone.

Even with restraints on its snout and front legs, it managed to escape. At 3:00 a.m., in the middle of a torrential downpour, Carmona and the security guards had to find the crocodile before it could make its way to one of the deeper water hazards and drown.

After an hour of searching they found the croc sliding on its belly toward a neighbor's swimming pool.

By the time the golfers showed up for their tournament later that morning, the storm had stopped, the crocodile was relocated, and Chloe had joined the Carmona household. 🐾

Chloe's Brush with the Law

It was a beautiful day in paradise and Mary decided to take four-month-old Chloe for some fresh air. She called her friends at Playa Royale and a day at the beachfront condos was arranged. Carmona transported Mary and Chloe in their *Critter Car*, a 2003 Volkswagen Pointer Sedan with upholstery that's been perforated with tiger teeth and claws. Even though it is Carmona's car—and Paradise Village's tiger—Mary doesn't have the permit needed to drive Chloe on public roads.

Carmona cautioned that Mary and her friends were free to play with Chloe as long she was on Paradise Village/Playa Royale property. However, she was never to take Chloe off the property.

Mary agreed.

What she didn't realize is that even though Playa Royale is right on the beach, the beach itself is public land.

Mary put Chloe on her leash and then she and her friends enjoyed watching Chloe romp around in the afternoon sun. Beachgoers were delighted to see a forty-five-pound tiger cub playing on the sand, and many snapped pictures or took videos.

But one beachgoer wasn't so thrilled. She called the police and reported a wild tiger running loose. From the panicked nature of the call, the police assumed one of Paradise Village's big tigers had escaped and was running rampant.

Word reached the beach that the police were called. In a panic, Mary and her friends took Chloe into one of their condos. As far as they knew, they'd done nothing wrong. They figured the police just wanted to maintain a presence. They stayed inside for about an hour, until the coast was clear.

Mary was shaken and wanted to get Chloe back home, but she didn't want to call Carmona and ask for transportation. Desperate times called for desperate measures. One of her friends brought her car to the lobby door. The others wrapped Chloe in towels, smuggled her into the car, and climbed in. As they pulled out of the gates, they were greeted by the flashing lights of federal, local, and transit police.

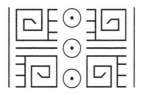

Mary, her friends, and Chloe were taken into police custody. All the women—still in their swim suits—were either American or Canadian, and none were fluent in Spanish.

That's when Mary had to make the most unpleasant phone call of her life. She had to inform Carmona that his tiger, his wife, and her friends were at the police station.

When Carmona arrived, he was able to clear up the misunderstanding and get Chloe and the women released. The police apologized for the trouble, explaining that they were forced to act when they thought there was a three-hundred-pound adult tiger on the beach.

In the end, every police officer got his picture taken with Chloe, and Mary learned a valuable lesson about public lands. And it's suspected that Chloe has a mug shot in the Puerto Vallarta police files. 🐾

Chloe's Identity Crisis

Chloe made new friends easily.

Chloe was no more than two hours old when she was rescued
from her mother's jaws. Not yet able to see and barely able to walk, she
entered the Carmona household frightened and confused. Like so many
rejected cubs before her, she spent her nights snuggled in bed with her
human parents. During the day, she slept in a box in the living room,
cuddled up with a stuffed, brightly-colored Tigger golf club cover.
     Within weeks she had a neighbor's cat as a playmate, but quickly
outgrew it. Next came the small dog that lived in the condo complex.

106

Chloe (in the blue harness) has her first face-to-face tiger encounter.

Once again, she outgrew her playmate in size and strength, so she went on outings with Mary, or stayed in Carmona's office at the golf course, happily playing with humans.

When Chloe was four months old, it was time to introduce her to her own kind. Carmona arranged a one-on-one tiger encounter for Chloe and one of the new cubs. Chloe sat motionless, eyeing the cub suspiciously until it was removed. Clearly tigers were not her favorite species.

Lluvia, the tigress that had rejected her, now had her second litter of three cubs and had accepted all of them. Carmona packed up Chloe in the golf cart and took her out to see the cubs.

Chloe, in her collar and leash, stood next to Carmona and stared at the tigers in the cage. When the three cubs noticed Carmona and Chloe, they toddled over to get a closer look. Chloe stiffened up and backed away from the cage. She tugged on the leash until Carmona released it, then she ran to the golf cart and hid behind it. No amount of coaxing could get her to come out in the open again. Whatever these strange, striped creatures were, Chloe wanted no part of them.

At seven months, she befriended a black Labrador retriever who liked to swim with her, though she found his barking and lunging invitations to play a bit unsettling.

When she was eventually moved to her own cage at the hotel, she spent hours on top of her waterfall, peering into the next cage to watch Diego and Daisy with a mixture of confusion and curiosity.

When Carmona and Chloe had their afternoon swim, the neighbor's
black Labrador retriever joined them.

The dog and tiger swam together for about ten minutes.

Living in a Fish Bowl

Paradise Village is a busy, year-round resort, and some of the tiger cages are located right in the center. People going to the hotel's towers, the mall, or the Spa Palenque walk right past them. Usually this is a good thing for all concerned; the people can watch the tigers, and vice versa. However, there are times when visitors' prying eyes can be a little…awkward.

The worst problems of living on display seem to arise at feeding time. Most of us are no longer closely related to our food sources. Our meat comes home on a styrofoam tray covered in plastic wrap. Many people are uncomfortable watching a television documentary showing a tiger tearing into an animal carcass, even though it's a true depiction of life in the wild. The tigers at Paradise Village eat entire animals—hide, bones, hooves, and all—which can be a shocking sight to onlookers.

These Bengals have food delivered to their den boxes. As with tigers in the wild, they're more comfortable eating in a hiding place. When the food stays in the den box, everyone is happy. The zookeepers have less area to clean, the tigers eat undisturbed, and the human visitors don't have to witness the gruesome reality of an animal feasting on a dead carcass. However, Carmona recalls a couple of times when feeding time wasn't so genteel.

The first was when he was conducting a tour of important dignitaries. It was feeding time and Khan was in his den box. But the tiger ran into a problem even dental floss couldn't fix. After tearing chunks of meat off the neck of a horse, Khan apparently decided he'd rather eat the horse's head. When he sank his teeth into the bony face of the horse, his long, sharp canine teeth punctured the eye sockets, sank into the skull, and got stuck there.

As Carmona talked to his visitors about the tiger program, they all heard a terrible commotion in the den box. Before Carmona could investigate, Khan came straggling out with a severed horse's head stuck to his teeth. To everyone's horror, he dragged the head through the grass, swung it from side to side, and even tried smashing it on the

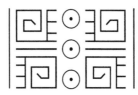

Chloe eating her favorite meal, chicken.

ground. The group watched in stunned silence until Khan managed to break free. Carmona is sure that no one in his tour group remembers anything he said that day, but he knows they remember their visit to Khan's cage.

Usually feeding mishaps are a result of the cats playing with their food. One of Lluvia's cubs marched out of the den box dragging part of a deer's leg. Another cub in the same litter nudged the deer's stomach outside the den box, then proceeded to pounce on it repeatedly.

113

The worst of these incidents happened at the hotel cages, when Diego had finished his meal of freshly slaughtered goat. He dragged the severed goat head out of the den box and happily threw it around. He used his paws to knock it against the cage bars, then he would bat it toward his pool.

At first onlookers stood silent and motionless, then all the children started crying. Carmona was called to the cages and told, "Make Diego stop playing with his food!"

Chloe Becomes a Working Girl

Three-month-old Chloe wants to drive the car.

Chloe's first couple months were like that of the other hand-raised tigers that had lived with Carmona and his wife. Tiger cubs start out sleeping fourteen to sixteen hours a day. Unfortunately, those hours are not all in a row. During the day, she would sleep in a cardboard box filled with towels and her Tigger. At night she would nestle between Carmona and Mary.

With the exception of the feeding/ burping/pooping/peeing/clean-up cycle that happened every three hours, life was peaceful. As she

grew, her bed was moved to the Jacuzzi bathtub, which gave her more room to sleep. Plus, the sides of the tub were too high and slippery for her to escape. The tub did double duty; it was also where she learned to swim.

For the first three months, she stayed home with Mary. They went for rides around the golf course, walks on a leash, and the cub entertained visitors with her antics. Like Carmona, Mary used these encounters to educate adults and children about tigers and our responsibility to help them.

At four months old, Chloe began sleeping in her crate. In the morning, Carmona greeted her with kisses and hugs, fastened her collar, and attached a long rope leash. After kisses and hugs from Mary, Chloe would hop into the golf cart and "go to work with Dad." Her days were spent sleeping in the shade, hunting lizards, and playfully stalking humans. Though she was raised by humans from the age of two hours old, her instinctive skill at sneaking up and pouncing on her unsuspecting victims was well-developed.

Some people brought toys for her. Not the cheap dog toys you get at the grocery store: the indestructible kind you give to Rottweilers. She spent a lot of time rearranging her possessions in her enclosure, dragging things from one corner to another.

Letting her have a bowl of water was asking for mud. Instead, the greenskeepers and pro shop workers had her on a bottled water schedule. Visitors were always entertained watching Chloe happily drink bottles of cold water every hour.

Her enclosure always had a couple of towels in it because she was obsessed with any fabric that dangled freely. This was due to a change in her daily exercise routine. Once she could out-sprint Carmona, he attached one end of a thirty-foot length of rope to her collar and held the other end. Then he tied a towel in the middle of the rope, and jumped in the golf cart. Chloe would stalk the towel, then pounce, but Carmona would move the golf cart, keeping the towel just out of reach. While this gave her better exercise, it also fostered her obsession with fabric.

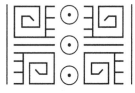

At five months old, Chloe preferred to wrestle with a towel than play with her heavy-duty toys. An unwitting visitor approached the enclosure with a denim jacket draped over her arm. Unfortunately, the visitor took her eyes off Chloe, and Chloe bit into the jacket. The tug-of-war over the jacket went from playful to insistent. The stubborn little tiger finally surrendered it, but only after time, patience, and three pro shop employees persuaded her to give it up.

After a long day of stalking visitors, it was time for Chloe to go home. Carmona fastened her collar and leash, and she jumped into his golf cart. About two hundred yards from the pro shop, Carmona pulled over for Chloe's designated potty stop. Then it was time for Carmona to leash walk Chloe the rest of the way home. In an undeveloped field just off the eighth hole of the golf course, Chloe jumped about, chasing butterflies and sniffing out bugs. She was comfortable on her thirty-foot rope lead, and never strained to go farther. She returned several times to Carmona for a nuzzle or a kiss, just the way a child will check in with a parent.

Carmona and Chloe walked onto a concrete path that led to the condo complex. Along the way, residents came out to greet them. A few who had small dogs on leashes waved, but kept their pets far away from the tiger. Workmen on a roof hollered down their greetings. As they walked by some roses, a very eager black Labrador retriever was waiting. The dog wagged his tail and barked an invitation to play. Chloe jumped back and hid behind Carmona. This was Chloe's swimming buddy, but his barking and clumsy enthusiasm often unnerved her. They proceeded to the pool where Carmona and Chloe had their evening swim. After they had a chance to relax and play in the water, the Labrador retriever was off lead and in the water, too. While Chloe wasn't fond of all his playful splashing, he had become the only playmate big enough for her.

After their swim, Mary met them with dry towels. Chloe's day was complete when she got her evening kisses and hugs, ate her dinner of raw chicken and pork chops, and settled in her crate for the night.

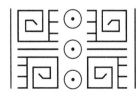

Chloe and the Paparazzi

Chloe rode to and from work with Carmona every day.

Because Chloe adapted so well to her work schedule, she was able to stay longer at the pro shop cage and enjoyed her rides to and from work in Carmona's golf cart. This didn't make her tame, she'd just learned to share her space with humans. But wild instincts are always working inside a wild animal.

One day when Carmona and five-month-old Chloe were riding home in their golf cart, they caught the eye of a photographer who was walking down the street. He began snapping pictures and following the

cart. As the cart began to pull away from him, the photographer started to run, snapping pictures the whole time.

That's when Carmona realized there was something wrong. Chloe had been watching the man and now sat tense and poised to pounce. Carmona knew that even with Chloe's thick collar and heavy rope leash, if the 120-pound tiger wanted to jump out of the cart, she would.

Big cats instinctively look at anything running away from them as prey. If it's chasing them, it's a predator. Either way, the situation didn't look good. Carmona grabbed Chloe's collar and held tight. He shouted to the photographer, "Stop where you are!" The man stopped and watched the golf cart come to a slow halt. Carmona braced himself in the cart and put both hands on Chloe's collar. "This tiger thinks you're chasing us. If she decides to jump out of the cart, I won't be able to stop her. You need to back away. Whatever you do, don't turn around or she will chase you. Just back away slowly."

The photographer stood motionless for a moment with his camera at his side. Then he slowly backed away. With every step, the tension in Chloe's body began to release, but she continued to stare at him until the cart pulled away and turned the corner.

A tiger, like any ambush animal, never wants a face-to-face conflict. If threatened, a tiger will fight, but it would much rather wait until your back is turned and then strike. Just stopping the photographer from running only solved half the problem. If the man had turned around to walk away, he would have triggered Chloe's ambush instinct.

In the Sundarbans, mangrove forests in India and Bangladesh, fisherman and loggers used this information to protect themselves from tiger attacks. They entered the area wearing face masks on the backs of their heads. This eliminated tiger attacks…for awhile. It seems the tigers figured out the mystery of the men with two faces and have learned to distinguish between the real face and the false one.

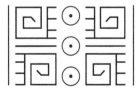

For Zoe

I have been at Paradise Village for the birth of several cubs, and my return visits have enabled me to watch Samantha, Khan, Diego, Lluvia, Daisy, and Chloe become adults. What a thrill it's been to see them: only hours old, taking unsteady steps at two weeks, ambushing lizards at four months, and finally entering their own adult habitats.

But on January 2, 2009, I saw a very different side of the people who work with the Paradise Village Bengals.

On that morning, holiday week visitors flocked to Lluvia's cage to see her four six-week-old cubs. But there was a different buzz among the employees. Sometime in the night, Samantha had delivered five cubs. Carmona, Dr. Cervantes, and Juan Diaz were concerned about the size of the litter. After all, Diego had been the rejected fifth cub in one of Casimira's litters. Within hours, the concern deepened; there were whispers that the fifth cub was sick. I went to Samantha's cage with my camera to see if I could get pictures of the newborns. Dr. Cervantes was sitting quietly inside a section of the den enclosure. He motioned for me to join him in his vigil, and I did. On the other side of the cage bars, Samantha lay with her cubs. We sat in the dimly lit enclosure, watched, and waited.

The tigress had chosen four cubs to nuzzle, wash, and guide to her teats. But the fifth cub lay just out of reach and Samantha refused to help it. At this point the cubs were about twelve hours old and had not been examined, weighed, or had their genders determined. Even more importantly, the vet wanted to help the rejected cub, but he couldn't reach into the den while Samantha was there. And she wasn't leaving. Dr. Cervantes stared at the rejected cub and shook his head. "Is there something wrong?" I asked.

He nodded sadly, "The legs."

I crawled over to the cage bars for a better look. The cub's front paws were tightly bent under her legs and the cub was unable to move. As the four chosen cubs nursed, Samantha closely watched our every move on the other side of the cage bars. The standoff continued.

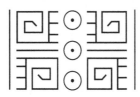

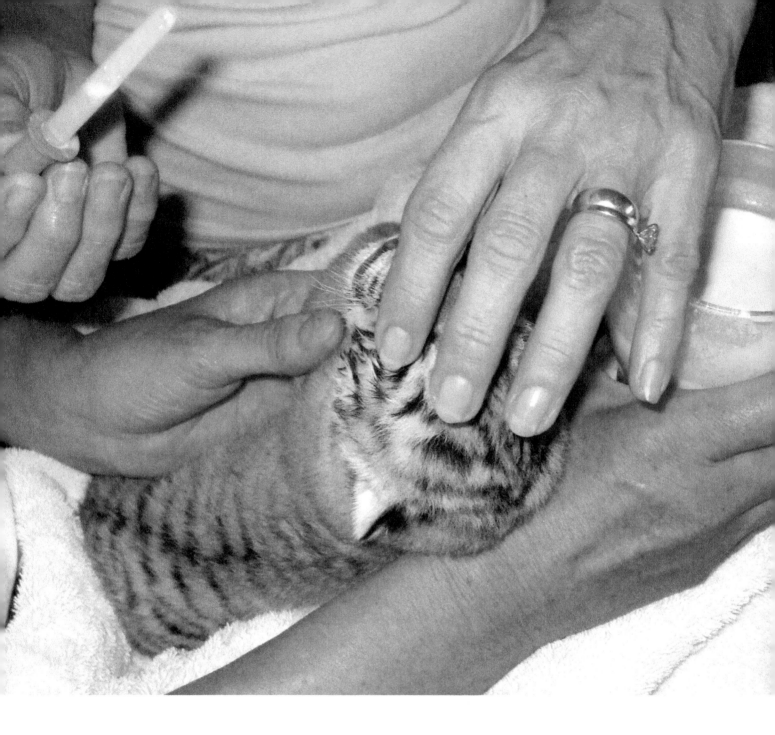

Mary Carmona, with Zoe in her lap, gives the cub her first meal.

At 3:00 pm, Samantha suddenly stood up and strolled into the afternoon sun. Dr. Cervantes quickly closed the guillotine door to keep her from returning. Opening another door, he crawled on his hands and knees into Samantha's den box. He sat cross-legged on the floor, picked up the rejected cub and carefully inspected it.

It was a girl, slightly smaller than the rest of the litter. He slowly extended her front legs. They softly collapsed back into their bent position. He cradled the little girl in his right arm and used the gloved

Dr. Cervantes removes Zoe from the den box and weighs her.

fingers of his left hand to check the formation of her skull. As if to himself, he whispered, "Her skull is not broken."

His thumb and forefinger traced her spine, stopping at each vertebra. "Her back is fine," he said, smiling.

He slowly stretched her front legs out again and put gentle pressure on the paws. When he stopped, the legs crumpled again. Cervantes shook his head and handed the cub to me through the bars. "Maybe...brain...."

125

While he went about his other tasks of weighing, examining, and identifying the three other females and one male in the litter, I held the fifth cub close to my heart and chuffed softly. She barely moved, and didn't make a sound: not a sigh, no muffled groan, and certainly not a robust cry like her litter mates.

A couple times she tried to lift her head but it flopped to the left side. Not a good sign. Her sucking motion—the first and most powerful instinctive motor skill—was barely there. Dr. Cervantes called Carmona, and then crawled through the walkway to the human side of the enclosure. With the pull of a cord, the guillotine door was raised, and Samantha re-entered her den. I was curious to see what her reaction would be when she realized a cub was missing.

She sniffed each of the four remaining cubs, washed them, then settled down to nurse. She never even missed the fifth cub that lay limp in my arms.

In a matter of minutes, Mary and her friend Trish pulled up in Mary's car as Carmona was getting out of his golf cart and entering the enclosure. I surrendered the little girl to Carmona who inspected her carefully, then tried unsuccessfully to extend the cub's front legs. He handed the cub to Mary who held it to her chest and stroked it softly.

Carmona and Dr. Cervantes spoke in Spanish to discuss the condition of the cub. Brain damage was mentioned. Death was mentioned. Then there was silence.

Carmona spoke to his wife, "Mary…take the cub home and feed her." He looked at me, "You go, too."

Mary, still cradling the cub, led the way to her car. Trish and I scurried to keep up. Suddenly there was a new, more forceful energy in Mary. "Don't you worry," she told the cub. "We love you and we're going to make you better. God still listens to prayers and he still grants miracles."

Trish and I stopped and looked at each other, surprised by Mary's transformation into a human tigress. Trish shrugged her shoulders

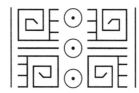

and smiled. "What better place to get a miracle than at *Jesus and Mary's* house?" We raced to catch up with Mama Mary and her tiger cub.

We entered the condo where a batch of tiger formula was mixed, heated, then poured in a coffee mug. Mary sat on the sofa with a towel across her lap and fed the cub with an eyedropper. After a couple eyedroppers full of formula we saw our first miracle; the little girl began to squirm and make muffled cries. After a couple more doses of formula the baby was awake, moving, and screaming like a healthy, hungry tiger cub should.

Since the cub had not been nursed the first twelve hours of its life, maybe all she needed was food. Maybe she was responding to the stimulation of being touched and held. Maybe she felt warm and comfortable. It didn't matter at the moment. The mood in the condo was jubilant as Mary massaged the cub's front legs, trying to get them to unfold. They didn't.

The three of us discussed the possibility of brain damage. Mary had seen it before, but her tigress resolve was unshakable. "If it's bad, then Jesus will take the cub tomorrow and have her euthanized. But tonight, she's going to be talked to, kissed, and cuddled. She's going to spend tonight sleeping on a pillow between us. She'll have food in her belly, and she'll know that she was loved while she was on this earth."

With that, Mary picked up the now-sleeping cub, kissed it softly on the face and cradled it in her arms. "She's going to know she was loved," she repeated.

By morning the cub had a name…Zoe. She was eating better and gaining strength. Dr. Cervantes had gone home that night and designed a cast that would effectively straighten her legs until she was strong enough to hold them straight on her own. Carmona contacted Mike Dulaney at the Cincinnati Zoo to help determine if the cub was brain damaged.

Hope mixed with caution was the mood around the tiger cages that day. Every hour Zoe survived was a major victory, another miracle. By late afternoon, I called Mary. "Is this the house of miracles?" I asked.

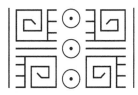

After a long silence, Mary answered, "She's dead." All the dashed hope, the denied joy, all the former celebration hung in Mary's voice like a weight.

I could only ask, "How?"

"She started going downhill. Didn't want to eat. I laid her down and stayed with her. I told her how much we loved her…and then she stopped breathing."

In the end, it was determined that Zoe was brain damaged. She was not destined to be a part of Samantha's litter or Carmona's family. But walking into the condo and seeing kitten formula and baby bottles in the kitchen, towels strewn on the sofa, and the familiar mop and bucket sitting unused on the tile floor shattered my heart.

Wishes unfulfilled, desperate prayers unanswered, miracles denied. Sometimes that's what you get when you play with tigers.

In an unmarked section of land in a place called Paradise is a burial ground. This is the resting place for all the tigers that have lived and died at Paradise Village. This is where the stillborns, the cubs who lived only a few short hours or weeks, and the adult tigers are laid to rest.

Little Zoe, quietly rejected by her mother, stayed alive long enough to know the feeling of food in her belly, nurturing strokes on her coarse fur, and peaceful sleep on a pillow between her human mom and dad. Zoe is here in this secret place. She joins Leoncio, the patriarch of this family: the rescued tiger from Guadalajara who started it all. 🐾

The Perils of Miscommunication

Ju-Ju with Chloe's stuffed Tigger hand-me-down.

Whenever any animal is brought into the Carmona household for rescue or rehab, Mary names it. Sometimes she doesn't even tell her husband—or anyone else—that the new critter has a name.

This was true of a little tiger cub Mary named Ju-Ju. The cub—one of Samantha's—had been born sick and was rejected by the tigress. Carmona and Dr. Cervantes had been working to diagnose and treat the cub, and it had started to rally. Mary, who had refused to leave the cub while it was sick, now felt able to leave the house. Her friend

Trish had twenty-five people meeting for Sunday brunch at the El Tigre Country Club and Mary gladly accepted the invitation to join Trish's friends and family.

Early Sunday morning, after Carmona left for work, Mary found Ju-Ju's lifeless body in the bathroom. It was the shock of the cub suddenly dying after such an encouraging recovery–added to Zoe's death a few months earlier–that devastated Mary. Sobbing, she sat on the bathroom floor and cradled the little cub.

Remembering her brunch commitment, she reached for her phone and called Trish to say she wouldn't be able to come. When she heard Trish's voice, she broke down. "Ju-Ju's dead! He must've had a heart attack! Oh God, I loved him so much!"

Now Trish, though she often babysits the cubs, had never heard the name Ju-Ju. That, plus the depth of Mary's despair, had to mean something horrific had happened. Ju-Ju must have been Mary's nickname for her husband, Jesus, Trish reasoned. Jesus Carmona was dead!

Trish hung up the phone and drove to Carmona's house, all the while calling people to cancel the brunch. She pulled up and saw no emergency vehicles outside. Was it possible she arrived before any first responders? She ran to the door, ready to help her friend cope with the loss of her husband.

Mary met her inside and began crying harder. Trish looked around the room for the body. There wasn't one.

Trish hugged Mary and asked, "Where is he?"

"He's in the bathroom," Mary sobbed. "I covered him with a towel. You can go see him."

Trish looked at the closed bathroom door, dreading what she'd find on the other side. "Are you sure you want me to go in there?"

"Yeah," sniffled Mary. "Go ahead." Mary looked toward the closed door and began crying again.

Trish walked slowly to the bathroom, took a deep breath to steel herself, then opened the door and peeked in. The little tiger cub, Ju-Ju,

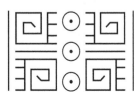

131

was lying on the bathroom rug partially covered with a towel. "Where's Jesus?" she asked.

"He's at work."

Trish turned around to Mary. "You mean, he's not dead?"

Mary shook her head. "No. Ju-Ju's dead. The baby. I named him Ju-Ju."

In short order, the tears became laughter as the two women realized the misunderstanding. Then Trish gasped and pulled out her cell phone. "Excuse me," she told Mary as she began dialing. "I have some calls to make."

For the rest of the day, as Carmona greeted people for Sunday brunch or walked through the pro shop, people stopped him to shake his hand and say, "Glad to see you're not dead."

Chloe is Transferred

Parents know the agony they feel when a child needs emergency medical care or a hospital procedure. Adults understand that sometimes pain is necessary to make you feel better, but the child often feels betrayed and abandoned. This was the case for Chloe's transfer from Paradise Village.

Chloe had been raised in a condo by human parents until she was old enough to be caged at Paradise Village. At first, she was content to dodge in and out of her waterfall, playfully stalking her toys—as well as passing visitors. But as she matured and became ready for breeding, she had hormones to deal with. She spent lonely days sitting atop her waterfall, watching Daisy and Diego play together. She became a mixture of cranky and listless, and she needed a mate. That's when Carmona realized they would have to say goodbye to her.

Paradise Village had only two males available as breeding partners: Khan and Diego. Khan is Chloe's father and Diego is her uncle, so neither male would be an acceptable partner. The Bengal program already supported four females and two males at a hefty annual price tag. Acquiring, caging, and supporting another male was not the best solution. If Chloe and her new mate fought like Kahn and Nala had, the breeding program would be back to square one, but with an additional male tiger to care for.

Carmona and Dr. Cervantes began checking every compound and zoo for a suitable location that would provide Chloe with a choice of breeding partners. In the Mexican state of Guanajuato, they found a private compound: clean and well-managed, with males ready to breed.

On Wednesday, January 26, 2011, Chloe would make the eight-hour ride to her new home in the back of Dr. Cervantes's truck. The drive would be the easy part. Getting her into her transport carrier and onto the truck was not only dangerous, but emotionally traumatic for Chloe and all the humans who had been involved in caring for her.

Moving tigers at a busy resort presents a huge safety problem when you're surrounded by tourists. The main risk is not a tiger escaping and running rampant through the property; it's a hundred visitors closing in on the area, upsetting an already-upset tiger, and

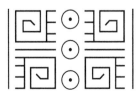

distracting workers with well-intentioned-but-constant questions. There must be silence and relative stillness so the humans can concentrate on their work.

The most dangerous part for the tiger is the use of anesthesia. A dose which would work under normal circumstances will have a lessened effect on an agitated tiger. Then the problem becomes how much more to use. What will be too much? It's an inexact science that can have deadly consequences for the tiger. Because of this danger, Carmona scheduled Chloe's removal at ten o'clock the night before the scheduled transfer. That way, most visitors would be in their rooms and the area would be quiet.

I arrived early to find Dr. Cervantes's truck parked by Chloe's cage. Cervantes was preparing Chloe's exit route through the side guillotine door of her holding cage. Juan Diaz and two other men talked quietly by the truck. Even though it was a beautiful, peaceful night, I could feel the tension in the cages. Chloe paced anxiously, watching Dr. Cervantes. Whenever he walked up to the side door, she would back away and pin her ears against her head. In the next cage, Daisy paced back and forth while Diego got up on his hind legs to peer over the wall into Chloe's cage.

Carmona and Mary arrived just before ten o'clock. More tension. Carmona knew what it was like to see one of his hand-raised tigers leave the property, but his wife Mary had never experienced one of her *children* being taken away. Carmona tried to get Mary to stay home, but she insisted on coming. As far as Carmona knew, he'd have two hysterical females on his hands. He told Mary to stay behind the truck, "Don't let Chloe see you," he warned.

Now, while Chloe paced in her cage, Mary paced on the far side of truck, muttering to herself.

With the exit route prepared, Juan, the workers, Carmona, and Dr. Cervantes grabbed the wood and steel transport carrier and hauled it to the guillotine door. Chloe watched them, pinned her ears back, hissed, and jumped up to the top of her waterfall. In the next cage, Diego lay panting and Daisy stood on alert: both tigers looking up at Chloe.

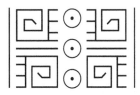

Dr. Cervantes walked around the corner and returned with a bucket of raw chicken, a tasty bribe for any tiger. Plan A was to use the chicken to lure Chloe into the transport carrier. She would see the food, walk through the holding cage and step right into the transport crate. Plan B involved a belligerent, uncooperative tiger and tranquilizer darts. No one wanted to think about Plan B.

Unfortunately, even though Chloe walked into her holding cage every day to eat, she wasn't about to do it now. It was Carmona's turn to try. He called to her until she jumped down from her waterfall and stood outside the holding cage, warily inspecting it.

After another fifteen minutes of coaxing, she stepped cautiously into the holding cage. The parrots in the cage beside her started squawking for all they were worth. Chloe turned and ran out of the holding cage before Dr. Cervantes could drop the guillotine gate. Now she was really suspicious.

The next attempt took forty minutes. Each time she approached the cage, the birds squawked louder. I was assigned to "talk to the birds" so they would calm down and quit screeching. Carmona held up pieces of chicken, coaxing Chloe into the holding cage. Mary, like a kid playing hide and seek, began to tiptoe around the truck: staying out of Chloe's sight, but getting closer to her.

Though no one wanted to do it, they finally had to resort to Juan's water hose. After several loud, defiant roars, Chloe was finally driven into the holding cage and the gate dropped shut. While everyone breathed a sigh of relief that Step One was completed, they were close to scrapping Plan A. Chloe was furious. She paced faster, and reached angrily through the bars at anyone who dared approach her.

Carmona hoped if they gave her some time to settle down, she would be okay. But she wasn't; she just became more frustrated and confused. Her chances of a safe dose of anesthesia diminished with every roar or charge. Furthermore, leaving her in this state of anxiety and agitation could cause a heart attack.

Carmona shook his head and walked back to the truck, tears in his eyes. Dr. Cervantes and Carmona decided that she would need to be

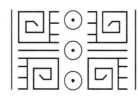

Working out of the back of his truck, Dr. Alberto Cervantes calculates the amount of tranquilizer to use in the dart gun.

tranquilized. Mary asked the men if she could please talk to Chloe and they consented. She walked to the holding cage and began singing all the children's songs she used to sing to Chloe when she was a cub. Such a strange tableau: a woman pressed up against a cage singing *Row, Row, Row, Your Boat* and *Patty-Cake*, while the tiger inside chuffed and moaned in response. For a brief moment it looked like Plan A might work; Chloe was calming down. But as soon as she saw any sight of her captors, she went into a rage again.

At the truck, Dr. Cervantes carefully measured doses of tranquilizer to load into the dart gun. I noticed that the minute the dart gun came out of its case, zookeeper Juan Diaz mysteriously disappeared. Knowing he'd been shot twice by a tranquilizer gun, I understood why. Carmona and Dr. Cervantes approached the holding cage with the dart gun. Chloe became enraged, charging at them and reaching her paws through the cage. Mary backed away. Now it was her turn to cry…and pray for Chloe's safety.

Dr. Cervantes took aim and shot. There was an angry roar from the wounded tiger, but Chloe was so upset, that the first dose of tranquilizer failed to work. Dr. Cervantes fired again. Chloe roared again, took a few steps then fell to the ground.

Carmona reached into the holding cage and placed a bath towel over Chloe's head to cover her eyes. Dr. Cervantes checked his watch, walked back to the truck to put the dart gun away, and picked up his stethoscope. Zookeeper Juan Diaz magically reappeared.

Dr. Cervantes walked cautiously into the holding cage and checked Chloe's heart rate. They waited for about ten minutes, then checked it again. By now, employees from maintenance and security had arrived to help move the tiger into in the transport carrier.

Carmona and Dr. Cervantes led the quiet procession of muscle power into the holding cage. They surrounded Chloe while Dr. Cervantes positioned himself at her head. He would back up into the carrier with her to make sure she was safe.

As the men lifted Chloe, her head jerked and she let out an angry roar.

I cussed, Mary kept praying, and the men froze in their tracks. Luckily, it was Chloe's last protest that night. Between the towel covering her eyes and the effect of the darts, she relaxed into a deep sleep. I later asked Dr. Cervantes if he was afraid when she suddenly woke up. He shook his head and smiled, "No. I trust the medicine." With the help of all the extra men, Chloe was gently placed in the carrier and the carrier was loaded into the truck.

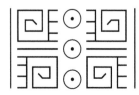

Her head covered with a towel, a tranquilized Chloe lies in
the holding cage under the watchful eyes of Dr. Cervantes.

A combination of the tranquilizing darts and the physical
exhaustion from her three-hour ordeal left Chloe sound asleep for
several hours, making her eight-hour ride uneventful. She now lives in
Celaya, Guanajuato, at a private compound that offered her a choice of
two handsome, healthy males: an orange Bengal and a white one. At
last she would have a mate. 🐾

The Ecology of Extinction

Some people take a very cavalier approach to extinction. They say that maybe a species has run its course. Maybe it's just nature's way of changing along with the planet. Time–and Man–marches on, and if an animal can't keep up, it's just a classic case of survival of the fittest.

We look at the skin covering our bodies as a borderline that announces, *I end here and the rest of the world starts*. But there is more to us than just the body-space we occupy. We need land for farming and ranching, materials for homes, as well as roads and waterways for shipping and transportation. As our population continues to grow, the Earth's resources shrink.

All of nature depends on balance. Each animal needs the proper food to eat, water to drink, and space to live. Should one of these resources disappear, the wildlife in that area will disappear. Once an animal is no longer part of that ecosystem, a link in the food chain is gone. The species beneath it can multiply out of control and the species above it has its food source disappear. As animals leave an area to find food, water, or land, more links disappear.

Today, we have the same amount of water as when the dinosaurs and saber-toothed tigers were here. We have essentially the same amount of land, too. But our planet is now home to seven billion people. Over a billion of them live in India alone. They need land to grow food and feed their families. The cities continue to build, making room for more people. That means forest land—the Bengals' home—is being cut down to provide housing. Deforestation changes ecological balances in the animal population, the soil, and even the air we breathe.

Animals are crowded into a smaller area, living on the edges of cities and towns. In India, farmers build huts along the boundary lines of tiger reserves. The men must harvest as much as possible to feed their families, so they farm on the reserve land, risking tiger attacks. Tigers wander out of the reserves and attack cows, which are easier prey than the sambar they usually hunt. To retaliate, the men hunt down the tigers to save their farm animals and their families. Everything falls out of balance.

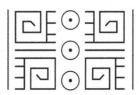

141

In the book, *The Way of the Tiger*, author K. Ullas Karanth cites population biologist Paul Ehrlich who likens Earth to an airplane. When a species becomes extinct, it's like losing a rivet in the wing of the plane. Threatened extinction is a warning sign that the environmental conditions on Earth are no longer in balance, and when a species disappears, the situation worsens. We can probably fly safely in an airplane missing a rivet or two. But if we fail to correct the problem, rivets will continue to disappear. Eventually, we will lose the rivet that is the last hope of survival for our ecosystem. Naturalist and author John Muir explained it this way, "When one tugs at a single thing in nature, he finds it attached to the rest of the world."

At present, we have lost three species of tigers to extinction: the Javan, Caspian, and the Bali tiger. The rest are on the endangered species list. Tigers are powerful predators at the top of the food chain, but they need forested areas, water, and a food supply. Man is the only animal who has the power to save the tiger by rescuing the environment.

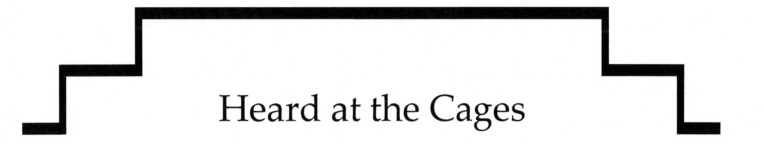

Heard at the Cages

Khan perched on the rock ledge above his waterfall.

Working in the Paradise Village Bengal Program means spending a great deal of time around the cages for care, feeding, and observation of the tigers. The following pages are a collection of the most frequently asked questions or comments that have been overheard by the staff.

"Where do they buy their tigers?"

Reputable facilities do not buy or sell tigers. This is all done solely for preservation of the breed.

When a tiger is born, flyers, E-Mails, and FAXs are sent to all reputable zoos and compounds who might be interested. The cub's birth date, weight, gender, and blood lines are included in these announcements. If a facility is looking for a breeding partner for one of its own tigers, they notify the cub's facility and begin all the paperwork.

The only money that is ever discussed is which facility will pay for transportation of the cub when it's ready to travel to its new location. Sometimes trades take place. It's even possible for two facilities to trade cubs in order to widen their respective gene pools.

When a tiger is three or four months old, it's time to relocate. The cub is eating meat and is no longer dependent on its mother for nourishment. Also, tiger cub mortality is at its highest in the first three months. Among the most common problems in cubs are strangulated hernias, seizure disorders, and kidney failure. If a cub makes it through its first three months, chances are very good it will survive in its new surroundings.

"It's a shame the tigers don't have any room to run."

Tigers don't run. Tigers are ambush hunters. They go to the nearest water hole, pick a shady spot in a bush, and wait for food to saunter by. They'll wait for hours.

A tiger waits until an animal's back is turned. The attack is so fast and deadly the animal doesn't have a chance to run. A tiger can leap forward fifteen feet from a crouching position. There is a YouTube video of a Bengal who leapt thirteen feet in the air to attack a *mahout* riding on an elephant. That Bengal had about twenty yards of running room before she was airborne and landed on top of the elephant's head.

A tiger's body is solid muscle and built for short, powerful bursts of energy. In the running world, they're definitely sprinters. If a tiger

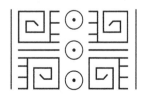

145

Hiding and ambushing are instinctive behaviors even rejected cubs exhibit.

has to run more than seventy-five feet to chase its prey, it will go hungry. Or even worse, its heart won't be able to keep up with the demands of its muscles and it can have a heart attack.

"Poor things. All they do is sleep."

If you have a cat at home, you've probably noticed the same thing. The answer to why they sleep all day is because they can. Felines are among the most adept hunters in the animal kingdom. Hunting takes very little effort or time for any kind of cat. Once that's checked off their to-do list, napping is about the only thing left. The rest of the animal kingdom has to roam the land, track down prey, chase it, and fight off the rest of the predators who want a piece.

There is also another reason why the Paradise Village tigers are sleeping; they play during the night shift. Bengals live in very warm, humid weather, but that doesn't mean they enjoy it any more than we do. The daylight is for shady naps or soaking in their pools. If you want to see the tigers play, you'll have to catch them before sunrise.

When the tigers are not playing with each other, they have toys to keep them busy. A large, specially formulated, hard plastic ball called a Boomer Ball can give them hours of fun. Before this virtually indestructible toy was developed, tiger cages used to contain sixteen-pound bowling balls for the same purpose.

During the fall, feline compounds will roll a pumpkin or two into a cage. Not only will the tigers bat it around, they take great pleasure tearing it apart. All large felines like the smell of cinnamon or nutmeg. Rubbing a pressed cardboard tube from a carpet roll with cinnamon, then giving it to a tiger will ensure hours of fun for the animal and visitors as well.

"Do tigers purr?"

When it comes to vocalization, the feline world is divided into two types: purring cats and roaring cats. The secret is in the hyoid bone, a small bone that connects the tongue to the cat's mouth. In your domestic cat, the hyoid bone is rigid. When a purring cat is relaxed, the air that passes in or out of the throat makes the hyoid bone vibrate. True purring happens whether the cat is inhaling or exhaling.

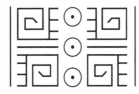

But your contented little fluff-ball isn't the only feline who purrs. The bobcat, lynx, and cheetah have the same vibrating hyoid bone. The largest of the purring cats is the mountain lion (also called the cougar or puma).

Tigers, leopards, jaguars and lions belong to a classification know as roaring cats. Their hyoid bone has elastic sections on either side; this allows them to roar when they exhale. If a true purr is defined as a sound that can be made on inhaling and exhaling, then tigers can't purr. But they can *chuff*.

Chuffing is a soft vibration of the vocal folds and a snort of air out the nostrils. A tigress and her cubs chuff at each other all the time. In tiger behavior, chuffing can be nurturing, comforting, loving, a sign of contentment, a greeting, or an apology.

"Are the tigers lonely?"

Tigers are solitary animals. They hunt alone, they live alone. The only exception is when a tigress has cubs. She will stay with her cubs for up to two years in some cases. But then it's time for the offspring to leave and find their own territory with a food source, water, and hiding places.

In Paradise Village, tigresses with cubs have allowed certain humans to share their cubs: particularly Carmona and Dr. Cervantes. When cubs are born, the mother will usually stay with them for twelve to fifteen hours. During this time she rests, nurses and cares for her brood. She is well aware that Dr. Cervantes is quietly waiting on the other side of the cage bars.

Eventually she gets up and walks outside her den box, leaving the cubs inside. Guillotine doors are closed to keep the tigress out and allow the vet to enter. He weighs them, determines their gender, and gives them a quick check-up. Then he slips back through to his side of the cage bars and the guillotine door is opened. The tigress returns, washes her cubs, and settles down to nurse.

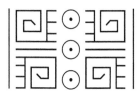

As the cubs get older, mom happily walks through guillotine doors allowing Carmona, the vet, or zoo staff members to enter. The tigress seems to consider it a little *me time,* and the cubs get a chance to interact with humans.

Since these cubs will be going to other zoos before their fourth month, the exposure to human sights, sounds, and smells makes them tractable. While tigresses in captivity seem to miss their cubs for a couple days, they also seem to quickly adapt and enjoy living alone again.

The tiger has maintained its solitary life style throughout the centuries. Its method of attack has allowed it to bring down prey that is bigger and heavier than itself with a single powerful strike that uses two bites.

Most people think all big cats attack with one bite to the jugular vein. The tiger's attack is different. The first bite is to the prey's larynx, taking out the vocal cords. That way the animal cannot cry out. A solitary hunter doesn't want its prey calling for help or, even worse, inviting an attack from a second predator in the area. The primary cause of death in a tiger attack comes in silent suffocation.

The second bite is to the jugular vein, which hastens the process. The tiger doesn't have to struggle with its victim; it just has to wait a few brief minutes until the animal is dead. Then the tiger drags its prey to a hiding place and feeds alone for three or four days on the carcass.

Tigers are quiet animals. They can roar, but don't do it often. Animals that hunt in a group, like a pride of lions, vocally communicate all the time. But tigers don't have anyone else to talk to and certainly don't want anyone to know they're around. Everything that is necessary to their survival is done quickly, quietly, unseen, and alone.

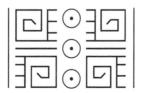

"What is the difference between a male and female?"

If you see two tigers sharing a cage, it's a good bet they're a breeding pair. This gives the observer a good opportunity to compare the male to the female. The male Bengal is larger, weighing between 425 and 500 pounds. The female Bengal is smaller, weighing from 300 to 425 pounds.

From birth, Bengal behavior can give you clues as to whether a cub is male or female. The males are larger, more aggressive, and impatient. They tend to enter the world loudly demanding food… right now! They tend to be more curious and do not like to be redirected when they are on a mission. Females, on the other hand can be very shy and wary of their surroundings. After a year or two, there are definite changes in these behaviors. The males become more docile and generally more predictable. On the other hand, the females become very unpredictable. Zookeepers attribute this to hormones, and most agree that the female's mood can change on a dime.

In most adult breeding pairs, the female is more likely to walk around, survey the grounds, and investigate anything out of the ordinary. The male will sleep or go for a soak in the pool. It's not unusual for the female to walk by a dozing male and give him a swat with her paw. Any conclusions about similarities between tiger and human behavior are purely up to the reader.

"Do tigers recognize each other?"

Yes. Scientists who document behavior on the reserves have discovered that tigers have excellent memories. Since tigers live alone, cubs leave their mothers to find their own territory. If they stumble onto each other after years of separation, they recognize each other.

Their memory is not only triggered by sight, but also by the sense of smell. Tigers notice subtle changes in markings of other animals. In the wild, a female in oestrus (heat) increases spraying activity. Males

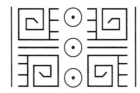

not only take notice of that fact by sniffing trees and turning leaves over, they remember if they have mated with that female before.

In captivity, tigers use their senses of smell and sight to identify people from whom they've been separated. The reaction to your reappearance will depend on your past relationship with that tiger. You see, tigers not only remember the people they like, they also have the ability to hold a grudge forever.

If a cub is rejected by its mother and is rescued from the cage and successfully raised, there will never be a happy mother/child reunion. Once the cub is rejected, it will always be rejected. A tigress apparently does not change her mind. Chloe could never share a cage with Lluvia. Just as Diego, Lluvia, and Nala could never have shared a cage with their mother, Casimira.

If you are mean or mistreat a tiger, there is no forgiveness: only revenge. And it will wait patiently for its opportunity to exact that revenge.

On the other hand, if you have been kind and nurturing to a tiger, they will forever remember that kindness. You can see this at the cages when the tigers get to see their favorite people. Diego's reaction to Carmona arriving for a visit has always been heartwarming. The afternoon is filled with playful energy and loving chuffs as his human dad pets him through the bars.

When Chloe was first in her cage at the resort, Mary Carmona went away for six weeks. When she returned, Chloe bounded back and forth in the cage, jumped in her pool then ran, soaking wet, to Mary for kisses and chuffs.

Khan, Lluvia, Daisy, and Samantha all come to the side of the cage to see Carmona when he visits. They put their faces up to the cage bars and chuff at him while he pets their faces or scratches their backs.

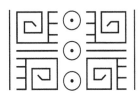

"They all look alike. How do you tell them apart?"

There is a saying, "You can tell a tiger by his stripes." That's true. You can even tell different subspecies of tigers by their stripes. Siberian tigers have brown stripes to match the surrounding bushes and trees. The other four subspecies have black stripes, but the number differs with each subspecies. The South China tiger has the greatest amount of stripes, followed by the Bengal, then the Sumatran tiger. The Indo-Chinese tiger has the least amount of stripes, and they don't extend all the way around the body.

Siberian tigers have a muted orange color that can range from tan to gold, with a great deal of white on their chests, underbellies, face, and legs. These colors allow them to blend in with the snow in winter and the brown landscape in summer. The Indo-Chinese, South China, Sumatran, and Bengal tigers have a more vivid orange color and less white than the Siberian. In addition, the adult Paradise Village tigers have the fuller white ruff or fringe around their faces, which is an adult Bengal trait.

Technically speaking, the markings on a tiger's face are like a human's fingerprints: both are not completely accurate but they will be close enough to make a positive identification. In addition, Carmona, the vet, and the zookeepers know the tigers by their coloring, behaviors, how they walk, their body structure, and their personalities.

Daisy has a lighter coat than the other tigers, because she's half white tiger. Diego has the traditional orange color, but in addition to the white on his ruff, he also has more white on his chest and neck. Lluvia has a great deal of white on her face and very striking facial stripes. On Samantha's right side, two of her black stripes intertwine like a chain.

Samantha carries herself with a smooth, regal walk. Khan—when he isn't neck-deep in his pool—likes to rest on the highest perch he can find.

Chloe was playful and loved to ambush. If a visitor turned his back on her, she'd sneak right up to him.

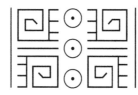

Just as mothers of human twins can tell them apart, it's a matter of being with the tigers every day to learn their differences.

"What's that smell?"

When you've visited the tiger cages, you may have noticed a pungent smell. Tigers are very territorial. In the wild, when a tiger finds an area with shade, hiding places, water, and enough food supply, he— or she—begins actively marking territory.

Tigers will back up to trees and spray a potent combination of urine and oily, scent-gland secretion. The oil and urine combine in a gummy film that doesn't rinse off with rainwater. In fact, zookeepers have to clean off accumulated spray with putty knives and lots of scraping.

In Las Vegas, Siegfried and Roy's Secret Garden compound features several white tigers. The zookeepers frequently rotate the tigers to different cages and the first thing a tiger does in his new cage is walk the perimeter spraying everything to establish his territory in his new location.

In Paradise Village, Diego has taken a more detailed approach. He has learned to share his cage space with his breeding partner, Daisy, but sometimes he gets tired of her playfully batting him around. He will choose two trees in his cage, spray both of them, then lie down between the trees for a long, hopefully uninterrupted nap.

A tigress in oestrus will do a lot of spraying not only to announce her presence, but to inform any passing males that she's ready to mate. Her spray also contains hormones that are only present when she's in heat. Males tend to spray more: anytime they think their territory is being threatened.

Which brings us to the greatest danger at the Paradise Village tiger cages. The cages were designed so you could safely see a Bengal a few feet from where you're standing. However a tiger can spray twenty-five to thirty feet. And you don't smell like his territory. That puts you in the line of fire, so to speak.

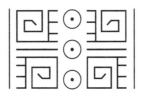

The claws of a three-month-old tiger already mean business.

If a tiger saunters over to take a closer look at you, he's also checking to see if you belong to him. He may decide you're a piece of territory he forgot to mark. If he turns his back to you and lifts his tail, you're about to get wet. Don't run backwards; you'll never make it. Just quickly dodge to the side about five feet. You don't want to spend part of your vacation scrubbing that stuff off your skin and out of your clothes.

"I heard they declaw their tigers? Why?"

The battle lines have been drawn on this issue. In Britain, you can't declaw your housecat. In the United States, declawing is up to owners and caretakers whether we're talking about a housecat or a Bengal tiger.

After researching different veterinarians and zookeepers, it seems the real issue is the botched jobs done by improperly trained people. In these cases, animals are left crippled and in constant pain because their paws have been mutilated.

Paradise Village Bengals are declawed by four months of age. The procedure is done with an accomplished professional using state-of-the-art laser techniques practiced in the United States and other countries. The veterinarian performing the operation has been overseen by others in the fields of animal science and zoology. It's performed at great expense and with the utmost care. In Chloe's case, she went to the vet in the morning and was released that afternoon.

Cubs that are to be placed in other zoos are transported before their fourth month to allow those zoos the declawing option.

For the cubs staying in Paradise Village, the claws are removed to protect breeding pairs from injuring each other. Mating is a rough procedure and not for the faint of heart. The male struggles to gain brutal dominance over the female. Even without claws, Khan almost killed Nala in an unsuccessful pairing.

It's the choice of this breeding program to remove the claws and lessen any danger to an already endangered species.

"What do they eat?"

In the wild, Bengals prefer to eat ungulates. That's the fancy, scientific word for animals with hooves. Their first choice is sambar, a species of deer. But they will eat any deer, goat, horse, cow, or even pig.

Their diet in captivity, which is weighed and measured so they won't overeat, is much the same. Farmers sell deer, goats, pigs, cows, and horses to be butchered and delivered to the cages. The Paradise

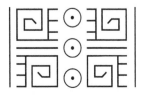

155

Though Lluvia's food is delivered to her den box, she often drags it out into the open to eat. This behavior is only seen in captive tigers who are not afraid of other predators taking their food.

Village tigers not only get the meat while it's still on the bone, they get it while it's still covered in skin. This gives them the closest meal to a diet in the wild.

The cubs get a different diet. They live on mother's milk for about six weeks. Then the tigress begins to pull meat off the carcass of her food, chew it, then transfer it to each cub's mouth. Every day she chews it less, until the cubs are happily tearing off pieces of meat for themselves.

The only one who didn't adapt well was Chloe. She transitioned from baby bottle to fresh chicken pieces and pork chops. The first time she was confronted with a carcass she decided she wanted to hold out for her nicely prepared chicken and pork instead of gnawing through hide and hair. It took a while to break her of her gourmet cravings.

"That tiger looks sick!"

Paradise Village received a negative review on a popular travel website claiming that they were mistreating one of their tigers. The blogger stated that the animal was moaning, groaning, and rolling around on the ground, obviously in pain. I happened to be visiting the resort at the same time, so I saw what the blogger saw. Daisy, the tigress chosen to be Diego's breeding partner, was in oestrus for the first time.

It was quite a disturbing show for the uninitiated, but after having volunteered at Rosamond's Exotic Feline Breeding Compound, I had seen it before. If you think your housecat is unbearable when she comes into heat, you haven't seen anything. When a big cat comes into oestrus, you don't know if you're watching a cruelty-to-animals exposé or a porn film.

Poor Daisy writhed around on the ground. She'd push all of her weight with her back legs as though she was powerless to get up, and considering tigers are quiet animals, she made quite a vocal fuss. But this is the fuss a tiger in oestrus makes.

Dr. Cervantes, Juan Diaz, and Carmona took turns visiting the cage and monitoring Daisy's venture into adulthood. Unfortunately about all you can do is let nature take its course. And find a way to explain it to the kids who are watching.

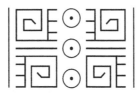

157

Carmona visits Daisy through the cage bars, as he does with all the adult tigers.

"What happens if the tigers get sick?"

The adult Paradise Village tigers have never left the property for medical treatment. There are two reasons for this. First, when a four-hundred-pound tiger is sick or injured, it will still have to be anesthetized an additional time just to transport it. The better option is to move the necessary equipment to the property.

Secondly, there have been only three people who have a permit to transport any of the tigers: Carmona, Don Graziano, and Dr. Cervantes. But even they are not allowed to take a tiger out of the state of Nayarit. Unfortunately, the X-Ray and ultrasound machines, as well as the as the laboratories suitable for testing a tiger, are located in Puerto Vallarta, in the state of Jalisco. The tigers may live minutes from the state line, but it may as well be hundreds of miles.

When Nala was brutally attacked by Khan, Carmona and Dr. Cervantes ordered an X-Ray machine, ultrasound, lab work, and all the necessary medical supplies to assess Nala's injuries and sew over four hundred stitches in her neck. All the supplies and machinery were rushed from Puerto Vallarta to Nala's cage, since Nala couldn't be taken across the state line for treatment.

"Does anyone go in the cages with the adult tigers?"

No. Not to socialize, play with, or train them. Even the rejected cubs who have been raised in Carmona's home are not tame. The tigers have a certain amount of trust and familiarity with Carmona and the staff. While that translates to warm greetings and friendly chuffs, it doesn't mean they are tame. It means they are tractable. They are still wild animals who have the power to seriously injure or kill without meaning to.

When Diego sees Carmona walking toward the cage, he is visibly excited. Carmona steps into a smaller, covered area and pets Diego through the bars. Diego's first move is always to jump up and try to put his paws on Carmona's shoulders like he did when he was sitting in Carmona's lap years ago. Except Diego weighs 450 pounds now. As Carmona says, "He'd break my back in a heartbeat."

During an emergency, like Chloe's surprise birth and subsequent rejection, a zookeeper kept Lluvia at bay with a water hose while Carmona rushed in to retrieve the newborn cub.

As is true with most compounds and zoos, there is a healthy respect for the power of the animal in the cage. Even cage cleaning

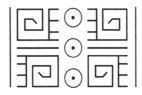

is treated with the utmost concern for the safety of the animals and humans. Walking into a cage, even when the animal is contained is deadly, serious business.

"Who's ever heard of a cat liking water!"

While it's true that most cats aren't fans of water, tigers need it to survive. Because of a tiger's dense muscle mass and heavy bone structure, it doesn't take much movement to raise their core temperature.

Zoologists figure that all tigers started from cold climates and, over the centuries, migrated to the warmer jungles of India and other parts of Asia. Unfortunately, their bodies haven't evolved to deal with the heat. So they have adapted by spending the hottest part of the day submerged up to their heads in lakes, streams, and watering holes.

The Paradise Village cages have pools so the tigers can cool off, or spend time playing in the waterfalls. Even rejected cubs get their chance to swim in Carmona's swimming pool. Water encounters usually start at two months. However, Carmona started one rejected cub at two weeks old, by holding it in his hands and letting it float.

To his surprise, the cub fell asleep. Or at least that's what Carmona thought. After this happened a couple times, he contacted Mike Dulaney at the Cincinnati Zoo. It turned out that the floating sensation made the cub feel like it was back in the womb, and it regressed to an unconscious state.

Swimming lessons were delayed for a few more weeks.

"If tigers like water, why do they run from the hose?"

The first surprise is observing a tiger like Kahn immersed to his neck in water, or seeing Daisy sitting under her waterfall. If they like water so much, how can they be repelled by a simple water hose?

The key to this answer is control…or the animal's lack of it. Even though tigers don't mind having their bodies wet, they're not crazy

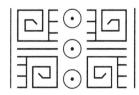

Chloe goes for a swim in the water hazard on the first hole of El Tigre Golf Course.

about water splashing in their faces. Khan entering his pool is quite a production:

- Front paw in water
- Take out front paw and shake it
- Put paw on rock and look around
- Turn around and put back paw in water
- Take out back paw and shake it
- Place back paw on another rock

- Slowly back into the water, stopping frequently to look around and adjust position

Honestly, my grandmother took less time getting into a pool. But even though my grandmother loved the water, if you came after her with a garden hose, she'd run the other way.

The night that newborn Chloe was rescued from her mother's jaws, there was a torrential downpour. Yet, spraying Lluvia in the face with a garden hose made her drop the cub and back away so Carmona could enter the cage and rescue the newborn.

The night Kahn attacked Nala in a fierce display of power during attempted mating, it was a regular old garden hose that drove him away and saved Nala's life.

The other time the tigers see the garden hose is when they're unwilling to be locked in their den boxes while the zookeeper and his staff clean the cages. The combination of the hose and someone demanding the tigers do something they don't want to do can create an interesting love/hate relationship between the zookeeper and the animals.

The tigers will happily greet members of the staff with gentle chuffs and lean into the cage bars to be petted. But when that same person walks up to the cage with a hose, it's a whole different story.

Just like it would be with my grandmother.

"Look! That tiger's making a funny face!"

The first day I saw the face I laughed. I was watching Lluvia as she tended to her three-month-old cubs. One had just urinated in a corner outside the den box and walked away. Lluvia saw the puddle, strolled over to it and thrust her nose in it to smell. She immediately raised her head, stuck out her tongue, and grimaced like a kid eating grapefruit.

That "icky face" is called a flehmen response. All felines, from tigers to leopards to your kitty at home, do the same thing. A feline's sense of smell is very powerful, but they also have a secondary way to

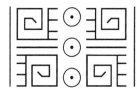

162

Diego exhibiting a flehmen response after sticking his nose in Daisy's urine.

detect specific odors. It's called the vomeronasal organ or Jacobsen's organ.

This organ helps them detect hormones and pheromones in urine. With this scent information, they can tell if a female is in oestrus, if another predator has wandered into their territory, or if it's urine from nearby prey. The Jacobsen's organ can tell them if the urine is fresh or days old, and give them information on the physical condition of the animal that left it.

But it's getting the scent back to the Jacobsen's organ that causes the funny face. A tiger pushes its tongue out of its mouth, opens wide, wrinkles its nose, pulls all the flesh up off its teeth, then breathes in the microscopic scent particles so they can pass over the Jacobsen's organ. We get to see a funny face; they get information that is important to their survival.

Felines aren't the only animals who exhibit the flehmen response. Ungulates like horses, sheep, and deer also have a Jacobsen's organ and demonstrate the flehmen response.

"How do you know when a tiger is pregnant?"

You don't. It's possible for a tigress to carry cubs to term and no one even spots a baby bump.

The obvious answer is to test the tigress, but testing means giving her anesthesia to do the test. While tigers are impressively strong animals, their systems are delicate. Think of a tiger as an expensive race car. It has lots of power but it has to be maintained more carefully.

The only clue zookeepers have is evidence of mating. This might include blood in the cage, bite marks, or tufts of hair lying around. When a zookeeper finds evidence of mating, the date is logged and projected forward 93 to 115 days for possible due dates. Of course, it's just as likely the tigress isn't pregnant, but all mating signs are taken very seriously.

While tiger mating isn't moonlight and roses, and there are usually signs of struggle, sometimes even that isn't dependable. Lluvia carried Chloe to full term and no one knew she was pregnant. That's why the Paradise Village tigers are watched around the clock by zookeepers and security.

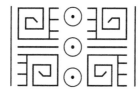

Three-month-old Nancy spent her days resting next to her father, Khan. Even though he was separated from his cubs upon their birth, he managed to form a bond with his daughter.

"Why doesn't the male tiger get to stay with the cubs?"

In the wild, the job of the male tiger is to impregnate the female then move on to another female's territory. Work, work, work. Keep moving along.

Some reserves have noted that the occasional male will stay with a female and her cubs for up to eighteen months. But they each have their own internal clock that tells them to move on. In the wild, nothing

165

prevents them from moving on. In a cage, they are trapped. This can lead to the males killing the cubs. It wouldn't be much of a preservation effort if the male killed all the offspring, so males are separated from the tigress and her cubs as soon as the cubs are born.

Khan has bonded with some of his offspring, but from the neighboring cage. One of Lluvia's litters produced a very shy *daddy's girl* who wanted to spend her time with Khan. He would rest against the bars on his side of the cage and she would lean against the bars on the other side.

Once the cubs have been relocated, the male and the female breeding pair can be reunited.

"What happens if a breeding pair doesn't get along?"

It happens. It's not pretty and it's life threatening.

Nala, a fiesty little tigress born to Casimira and Leoncio was placed in a cage next to Khan to see if they would be compatible. Everything looked great. Time for the second step: supervised meeting.

Nala and Khan were put in the same cage under the watchful eye–and ready water hoses–of Carmona, Dr. Cervantes, and Juan Diaz. All went well; it looked like Khan would have a new mate.

However once Nala came into oestrus and Khan made his move, everything fell apart. Nala violently refused his advances. Khan retaliated with strength and force that almost killed her. Before the staff could drive him away with the hose, he had torn off chunks of her scalp and ripped into her neck in his attempt to subdue her.

Mind you, this happens in all breeding compounds at one time or another. And it happens in the wild. The only difference is that in the wild, it would be a fight to the death.

It took four hundred stitches, months of constant care, and lots of money to heal Nala. As with other compounds and zoos, there is always the hope that the second time—if there is one—will be the charm. Many times that is the case. The female will return to the male and they'll be a

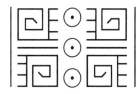

compatible breeding pair. But it quickly became apparent that Nala was not going to cooperate.

With Lluvia approaching breeding age, it was determined that Samantha and Lluvia would share Khan as a breeding partner, which was a successful arrangement. Once Daisy was ready to breed, she was placed with Diego, and she has been smitten with him ever since.

"What happens to tigers when they're too old to breed?"

This is where the real commitment starts. When a tiger is producing lovable little cubs, everyone is interested. People have been drawn to resorts and even shops because tiger or lion cubs are on the premises. But the day comes when the tigress is either physically or emotionally done producing cubs. If she is physically compromised, she will produce weak or stillborn cubs. If she is emotionally finished, she will begin to actively reject all of her cubs, choosing to kill them instead.

All three tigresses at Paradise Village, Samantha, Lluvia, and Daisy, are no longer breeding. They have certainly earned their rest after producing healthy cubs with strong bloodlines for zoos throughout Mexico. Now, what will happen to them?

Nothing.

They will continue to live here in comfort: eating quality food, staying in clean cages, and having access to expert medical help for the rest of their lives.

This is the real expense of a tiger breeding program. The average life of a tiger in captivity is fifteen years. A tigress may only be able to breed for half that time. As they get older, more medical problems will cause more expensive care and treatment, special food, and more medication to keep the tigers healthy. Zoos and compounds all over the world have the same challenge: giving their older animals the special care they deserve.

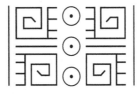

"Will they release any of these tigers into the wild?"

It's only natural to assume an animal preservation program would include eventual release into the wild. And that would be the ideal situation for any endangered species. Unfortunately, between the burgeoning human population, and our ever-growing demand for resources, there is very little *wild* left. World Wildlife Foundation estimates that the world's tigers have had their living space cut by almost half. And we only have five percent of the total tiger population we had in 1910.

The Sundarbans, the largest Indian/Bangladeshi mangrove forest, is also the world's largest home to Bengal tigers. An estimate of the world's wild population of Bengals is approximately 2100 tigers. The Sundarbans supports between 400 to 600 of those tigers. That's roughly twenty to thirty percent of the wild Bengal population.

With men coming daily to fish and chop down mangrove trees, the tigers have begun to kill humans. Understandably, the men now kill the Bengals to protect themselves or as an act of retribution.

It's a daily fight for survival in the Sundarbans, and the tiger is losing. The rest of the Bengal population—while protected by endangered species laws—falls prey to poachers who are looking for tiger body parts.

Until we do a better job of taking care of endangered species like the tiger, the only way to preserve them is to protect them.

Is captivity the most natural living situation for them? No. Is it the only one that will keep them safe and healthy? For now, yes.

Zoologists, zookeepers, and all the dedicated workers in animal science would like nothing better than to release all their caged animals into the wild. Unfortunately, it would mean illness, starvation, slaughter, and finally extinction for a great many species. So the caretakers have chosen the next best option; they operate zoos and compounds to educate the human population and hopefully inspire us to join them in animal preservation efforts.

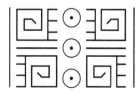

The Carmonas' Scrapbook
Fierce Predators

One of the best parts of my life was helping to raise baby tigers; one of the saddest parts was losing a tiger to illness and death. Through all those incredible years, the tigers brought me love, peace, and newfound friends.

For that, I will be forever thankful.

~Mary Estes Carmona~

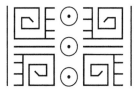

Author's Update, July 2015

This book has taken years to observe and record the Paradise Village Bengal Breeding Program. While the early 2000's were filled with the births of many cubs, the breeding is now complete. All the females are now sterile.

The cages on the far end of El Tigre Golf Course are home to Samantha, second oldest of the tigers; and Lluvia, third oldest and last of the Leoncio/Casimira bloodline. Khan, the next-to-youngest, shares the same cage with Samantha.

Once the breeding program finished, the humans who were instrumental in the survival of the cubs and the success of the program, took other jobs and have left Paradise Village. Only veterinarian Alberto Cervantes remains on the property. However, most medical emergencies in any breeding program happen because of mating, birthing, or weaknesses in young cubs. Older exotic felines in American zoos and compounds pretty much live out their lives in peace, just like these Mexican Bengals.

Don Graziano, the visionary who conceived of paradise as a place where Man and animals could live together, has relinquished most of his duties to his sons and daughter.

In March of 2015, Diego, the oldest tiger in residence, was diagnosed with cancer in his jaw. The Sovernigo family flew in a specialist from Mexico City to assess his condition and begin immediate treatment. In spite of all treatment measures, Diego lost his battle with cancer and was euthanized on June 8, 2015. The willingness of the Sovernigo family to give the best care and treatment to their oldest tiger is an encouraging sign that they will continue their father's passion for the Bengal tigers of Paradise Village.